Records of the
Militia
and
Volunteer Forces
1757-1945

Recruitment poster for the Cambridge Territorials 1909. (COPY 1/284)

PUBLIC RECORD OFFICE READERS' GUIDE NO. 3

RECORDS OF THE MILITIA AND VOLUNTEER FORCES 1757-1945

Including records of the Volunteers, Rifle Volunteers, Yeomanry, Imperial Yeomanry, Fencibles, Territorials and the Home Guard

Revised and Updated

BY

WILLIAM SPENCER

PRO Publications

DEDICATION

When I was a young boy, an old man, slightly bow-legged, used to come and mow the lawn at the house where I lived. This was 'Mo Mo'. 'Mo Mo' had fought in the First World War, although he would say very little about it. After I had experienced my war in the Falklands, he spoke of his own. Although our wars were different, we had both served our country, much as the men discussed in this book did.

GEORGE EDWARD HIGHAM
1/1 NORTHANTS YEOMANRY 1914-1918

PRO Publications
Public Record Office
Ruskin Avenue
Kew
Richmond
Surrey
TW9 4DU

ISBN 1 873162 44 8

CONTENTS

ILLUSTRATIONS

PREFACE TO THE SECOND EDITION

Since the first edition of this work by Dr G Thomas was published in 1993, a number of records, many dating from the First World War, have been released which may be of use to those tracing individuals in the Militia and other volunteer forces from the late nineteenth century to the early 1920s. This new edition also takes into account changes in the location of records and finding aids since the closure of the Public Record Office Chancery Lane site in 1996. Other sections have been expanded and new sections introduced, including detailed case studies for four soldiers who served between 1790 and 1905.

The decision to add a chapter about the Imperial Yeomanry was taken because of their importance in the changes which took place in 1901 and 1904 relating to voluntary service overseas. Although not technically Militia or regular army, the Imperial Yeomanry were soldiers who volunteered to serve overseas for a short duration only.

The large amount of manpower needed during the First World War generated many personal records of service. Many of the men who saw service between 1914 and 1918 were Territorials and former Militiamen, Yeomanry and Special Reservists, and until 1940 their records were largely intact. After the fire at the War Office record repository in that year many records were lost forever. The surviving First World War records of service for these men are discussed in a new chapter of this book.

My initial thanks must go to Dr G Thomas, much of whose text remains substantially unchanged, for his thoughts and advice relating to this second edition and various records over a number of years.

Thanks are also due to Mr A Lawes, Ms J Matthews, Mr M Prater, Miss M Skinns, Mr M Stainton and Mr E Tilley for their help in the production of this work.

My final thanks go to Kate and Lucy.

PREFACE TO THE FIRST EDITION

In times of national emergency, the Government has recognized the imperative of forming, in addition to the regular armed forces, a military capability dedicated to the defence of the Kingdom. By ancient practice, dating back to Saxon times, all able-bodied men between the ages of 16 and 60 were liable to perform military service within their counties. During periods of national emergency, under the Tudors and Stuarts, statute law had augmented the militia ranks[1]. From 1640, however, the latter were permitted to dwindle for the ensuing century.

This Readers' Guide takes for its point of departure the re-forming of the Militia in 1757, a measure taken by the Government in response to the dangerous military situation arising on the Continent in the form of the Seven Years War. While Britain herself was not directly threatened, the British monarch wore also the Crown of Hanover. Protagonist and antagonist in the Seven Years War were, respectively, Austria and Prussia; and the Kingdom of Hanover allied itself with France, the ally of Austria.

The records left by the various sections of the auxiliary military forces are scattered throughout a number of record classes in the Public Record Office (PRO). Even those records to be found in a single class are rarely arranged in any order that is meaningful to the user. One of the guiding principles that I have adopted has been the need to bring order out of chaos, and so of regrouping references to records of a similar nature or thematic content, and of imposing some discipline upon them, in order to make them meaningful. In that regard, I willingly admit, my regrouping of references may seem at times a little forced, if not arbitrary. Nevertheless, I remain satisfied that readers will now at last be able to find their way around a scattered and very defective collection of records. And with that aim in mind, I have not hesitated to use the same information under differing heads.

This Guide does not deal with the records of Colonial Militia.

The Imperial Yeomanry of the South African War (1899-1902), although containing in its ranks units of the Militia and the Yeomanry Cavalry, was neither Militia nor Yeomanry Cavalry, and its records are discussed in the PRO Records Information Leaflet 59 *British Army records as sources for biography and genealogy*.

Another guiding principle has been the recognition that an indication of the limits of survival of records is as useful to the researcher as knowing where to find the surviving ones. Moreover, although I have not deliberately set out to discover the whereabouts of records that may survive in collections not in the custody of the Public Record Office, where that information has come to my attention, I have included it, but without verification. In addition, and likewise without attempt at verification, I have suggested the reasonableness of seeking a given type of record elsewhere. The user is asked to differentiate between what is stated as fact, and what is suggested as being likely. References to records known to be in the custody of the Public Record Office are followed by a documentary reference number, eg WO 68/139, and with the abbreviation PRO in those instances where I deemed it needful. Most of these records are at the Public Record Office Kew. Where they are at the PRO Chancery Lane [now closed] this is noted in the text. Documentary references of records in other record offices are suitably identified.

As far as the concept of this guide is concerned, a great debt is owed to the work of Dr P Boyden of the National Army Museum[2]. His approach commends itself by its self-evident, rational simplicity: allowing the creators themselves of the files to tell us exactly what their work comprised and how much of it was set aside in safety for future generations. And it is certainly true that as well as discovering what source material the user has available to him, he needs to know when those sources begin and end and what their limits are.

My thanks also go to Dr A Knightbridge, Mr J Murray, Miss F Prothero and Mr M Stainton, for expert help in the production of this work.

---

[1] For a discussion of the records of the period that are in the custody of the Public Record Office, see PRO Records Information Leaflet 46 *Militia Muster Rolls, 1522-1640*, and for records deposited elsewhere, J Gibson and A Dell, *Tudor and Stuart Muster Rolls*, Birmingham: Federation of Family History Societies, 1989.

[2] P Boyden, *Regimental Records of the British Army, 1859-1900*, in: E T Rice and A Guy (ed), *Army Museum '87*, London: National Army Museum, 1988, pp 36-44.

Using the Public Record Office

The Public Record Office (PRO) is at Kew where original records are held.

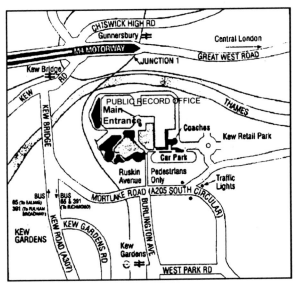

Public Record Office, Ruskin Avenue, Kew, Surrey, TW9 4DU.
The telephone number is:
0181-876-3444.

Hours of opening

Monday	9.30am to 5.00pm
Tuesday	10.00am to 7.00pm
Wednesday	9.30am to 5.00pm
Thursday	9.00am to 7.00pm
Friday	9.30am to 5.00pm
Saturday	9.00am to 5.00pm

Certain popular classes are viewed on microfilm, and some can be seen at the Office's central London microfilm reading room which is at:

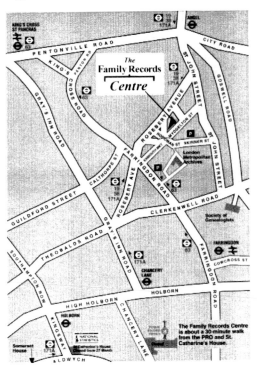

**Family Records Centre
Myddelton Street,
London EC1 1UW.**
The telephone number is:
0181-392-5300.

Hours of opening

Monday	9.00am to 5.00pm
Tuesday	10.00am to 7.00pm
Wednesday	9.00am to 5.00pm
Thursday	9.00am to 7.00pm
Friday	9.00am to 5.00pm
Saturday	9.30am to 5.00pm

The office at Kew is closed on public holidays and for annual stocktaking. The central London reading room does not close for stocktaking.

When you first visit the PRO, please bring with you formal documentary proof of identity bearing your name and signature. If you are not a British citizen you will need to bring your passport or national identity card. You will then be issued with a Reader's Ticket. Without a valid ticket you cannot be admitted to the reading rooms or order documents. You do not need one to visit the central London microfilm reading room.

You may use only graphite pencils in the reading rooms. Pens of any kind are not allowed. You may use personal computers, typewriters and tape recorders in designated areas. A full list of Reading Room rules is available on request.

Each document has a unique three-part reference. The first part is the lettercode, for example PROB for the records of the Prerogative Court of Canterbury or IR for Inland Revenue, according to the provenance of the documents, but with the growth of bureaucracy the letters given do not necessarily bear any resemblance to the body concerned, eg Council on Tribunals is BL. The second part is the class number, which represents the series within the lettercode. The third part is the piece number, which represents the individual document.

To identify the lettercode and class, consult the published Current Guide, which is the primary guide to the holdings of the PRO. The Current Guide is in three parts. Part 1 describes the history and functions of government departments. Part 2 briefly describes each class with information such as the covering dates and number of pieces. Part 3 is the index to the other two parts. There is no general detailed index covering records in the PRO. Once possible classes have been identified, the next step is to consult the class lists which briefly describe each piece. These are available in the PRO reading or reference rooms.

1. MILITIA (1757-1907)

1.1 Introduction

1.1.1 Creation and Evolution of the Militia

As a measure to counter the perceived threat looming on the Continent, the Militia Act 1757 was enacted to re-establish Militia regiments in the counties of England and Wales, a policy extended to face the threat arising from the American and French revolutionary wars, the Napoleonic Wars and, later in the nineteenth century, the Crimean War. Recruitment was by means of a sort of conscription, by which the 'Principal' or 'Drawn Men' were drawn by ballot from the lists of adult males (aged 18 to 50, 1758 to 1762; aged 18 to 45, 1762 to 1831) that each parish was required to draw up. The 'drawn man' could delegate his militia obligation to a substitute.

It is important to use the correct terms in identifying the various lists drawn up pursuant to that legislation. The lists of adult males created by each parish are known as Militia Ballot Lists; the more limited lists of men chosen from those Militia Ballot Lists are known as Militia Lists and the lists of men actually on the strength of a Militia regiment are known as Militia Muster and Pay Lists (WO 13) and Enrolment Lists (WO 68). No Militia List is known to be in the custody of the Public Record Office: such as survive are in the custody of the appropriate county record office, or in the case of Scotland in the record classes Sheriff Court (SC) or County Council (CO) at the Scottish Record Office (SRO). And some Militia records for Scotland may be found in the record class GD in the Scottish Record Office: eg the Seaforth Muniments include lists of men between the ages of 15 and 60 able to bear arms in parishes in Ross-shire in 1798 (SRO reference GD 46/6/45). The value of the two sets of Militia muster records to the military and social historian derives from a comparison made between them; their value for the genealogist and social historian lies in the fact that the lists constitute a national census of the adult male population during the latter half of the eighteenth century. Certain social classes were at first not listed (peers, clergy, teachers, apprentices and 'peace officers'), but a Militia Act of the following year, 1758, allowed of no exclusion. Subsequent Acts extended the amount of information to be included in the Militia Ballot Lists: they are the Militia Act 1802 and the Militia Act 1806. Some Militia Lists have been published through the good services of local history societies[1].

From 1794, lists of officers serving in the Militia were published by the War Office - see section 1.3 and **figure 4**.

---

[1] Eg W G Hoskins, *Exeter Militia List, 1803*, London and Chichester: Phillimore on behalf of Devon and Cornwall Record Society, 1972. See also the information on places of deposit in J Gibson and M Medlycott, *Militia Lists and Musters, 1757-1876*, 2nd edn, Birmingham: Federation of Family History Societies, 1990.

In 1825 discussion began concerning medical practitioners and the Militia ballot, and in 1827 they were granted exemption from it (WO 43/320). By 1827 questions had arisen concerning the legal liabilities of men drawn for Militia service pursuant to the Ballot Act, but disqualified from serving (WO 43/298).

For the regular Militia, a provision of the Militia Act 1757 authorized 'drawn men to arrange for substitutes'. In the case of volunteers, substitutes were not available since the men volunteered and there was no ballot; and so the legislation for the Supplementary Militia Act 1796 could make no provision for substitution (WO 40/9). Among the Militia Sub-Divisional Accounts for the year 1813 are records of fines paid for exemption from Militia service (WO 9/23).

The ballot was generally detested, and revolt against it became a cause of nervousness among members of the higher echelons of the Government. The situation was periodically 'monitored'; and that generated considerable correspondence, which is to be found in the officers' private papers, the majority of which are in the custody of the British Library and amongst other major repositories and private collections. The nervousness was particularly acute in Ireland, and with cause, for it was a combination of Militia and rebels that led to the rising on Easter Sunday 1799 (WO 1/693, f 131).

In Ireland, an additional dimension to the detestation of the Militia service and ballot lay in the local perception of the Militia as a measure of English, protestant domination, particularly as, in 1778, the Militia was constituted to be employed in 'suppressing insurrections and outrageous tumults and in pursuing, apprehending and attending the execution of notorious offenders' (Militia Act, Ireland, 1778). The Irish Militia was disembodied in 1802 (WO 43/400). It was further reduced in strength between 1822 and 1823 through the discharge of supernumerary sergeants, corporals and drummers (WO 43/190). The Solicitor General's report on the Irish Militia Bill, 1 July 1798, is in PC 1/43, bundle A148.

The records of the apportionment of the Scottish Militia for each county, April 1798, are in PC 1/42, bundle A141. On 26 November 1798, an Order was drafted for the calling out of the remainder of the Scottish Militia that had been balloted for: the draft, together with the Advocate General's report and the Order published two days later, is in PC 1/43, bundle A148.

Royal warrants of 6 September 1852 and of 8 December 1854 authorized Beating Orders, ie authority to recruit by drumbeat (WO 43/903). WO 32/21A (p 425) contains a memorandum on recruiting of the Militia, dated 1870. The raising of the Militia was a perennial problem: a file of 1807 contains details of the terms of service in the Militia and also the difficulties in raising it (WO 1/612, pp 119, 131, 147, 331), the same year that the Militia was augmented (WO 1/774, pp 67-185, 297, 393). The Selected 'A' Papers and Registers that have been placed in record class WO 41 concern the Militia,

Yeomanry and Volunteers, 1810 to 1822. To establish the contents of each year's record, the registers in WO 41/76-98 should be consulted.

Volunteering from the Militia to the regular army was carefully monitored by the military authorities to prevent the transfer of more than the acceptable quota. A record of the regimental quota for enlistment of militiamen into the regular army for the year 1803 is in WO 1/612 (f 189). In 1805 the Home Office issued a circular on the point (WO 40/23); and one of the questions figuring on the Attestation Forms filled in by regular army recruits challenges the latter upon that precise detail. On the other hand, militiamen who had fulfilled their Militia service obligations found favourable terms offered them on their transferring to the regular army (WO 40/23). A militiaman normally served three years, later five years, after which he could legally join the regular army. In some cases — particularly non-commissioned officers (NCOs) needed as instructors (WO 3/17), and, following the Militia Act 1796, a soldier or NCO on discharge to pension through Chelsea Hospital (WO 117) — he was authorized to join a local Militia unit on full pay (Militia Pay Lists, WO 13). In such cases the taking up of the awarded pension was postponed, an eventuality which was clearly countenanced in the Enrolment Books (WO 68). A militiaman was not attested for service overseas and could not so serve; in order to do so, especially during the period of the American Wars, he could transfer to the regular army; and it is then among regular army records that the research should continue. In 1799 the Irish Militia and Fencibles offered, however, to serve abroad (HO 100/83).

Certain records created pursuant to subsequent Defence of the Realm Acts risk being confused with the Militia Pay Lists (WO 13). They are the *Posse Comitatus* Lists of 1798 (Defence of the Realm Act 1797) and the Levée en Masse Lists of 1803-1804 (Defence of the Realm Acts 1803). In effect, those lists constitute additional censuses of the adult male population. But their original purpose was to establish a public list of men not already engaged on military service and who would be available for the purposes of civil defence in case of invasion. Surviving *Posse Comitatus* Lists are in County Lieutenancy records in the custody of county record offices. Levée en Masse Lists were retained by the compilers, and some subsequently have been deposited in county record offices along with the owner's private papers. Some have been published. Statistical summaries derived from these lists are in County Lieutenancy records and in Privy Council records.

As part of the general reorganization of the Army undertaken in the 1870s and which culminated in 1881, Militia units were attached to the appropriate county regiment as its third (and sometimes fourth) battalion. The new arrangement can be ascertained from the *Army List* of 1882. It is also set out in the introductory note to the listing of record class WO 68 and in Appendix 3 of this guide.

1.1.2 General Records

The Militia Regulations Made by the Secretary at War in pursuance of The Act 15 & 16 Victoria, cap 50; ... (London, 1853; also Sessional papers, House of Commons 1852-1853, 32, lix, 509 [PRO reference ZHC 1/2078 - available on microfiche in the Microfilm Reading Room]), specified the returns to be made to the Secretary at War by commanders of Militia units. They included four specified records of the annual training period, pay lists and monthly returns. Half-monthly returns of recruits and casualties were to be sent by the Adjutant to the Clerk of the General Meeting for the information of the Lord Lieutenant of the county. Of those returns, only the Pay Lists (WO 13/1-3393) and the Monthly Returns (WO 17/974-1002) have survived.

Regimental Books were not mentioned in the *Militia Regulations of 1853*, but seventeen were specified in the *Regulations for the Militia 1894* (HMSO, 1894). They included temporary and permanent regimental order books, records of officers' services, a letter-book, a digest of services and a sub-cash ledger. Each company was, in addition, required to keep four books, though no regulation governing their preservation or destruction was made. The War Office called them in, probably between the two World Wars, then deposited them in the Public Record Office, where they constitute the class of Militia Records (WO 68). However, not all were handed in. Some remain in private hands, others have been placed in regimental museums and county record offices. For example, Somerset Militia books from 1836 have been deposited in the PRO at Kew (WO 68/158-172), but the books prior to 1836 are at the Somerset Record Office, Taunton; Devon Militia books are at the Devon Record Office, Exeter, and the PRO holds only a digest of service of the 2nd (South Devon) Militia in WO 68/139. The conclusion is clear: some units are better documented than others, but all are documented badly.

The Attestations, which the *Militia Regulations of 1853* required to be preserved at regimental headquarters, have been deposited in the PRO, where they constitute record class WO 96. Their arrangement is by regiment, then by alphabetical order of militiaman's surname. They belong, however, in the main to the period 1870 to 1908.

A major source of information about the evolution of the Militia, the Volunteers and the Territorial Army, is constituted by the periodic returns made to Parliament and published in the *House of Commons Sessional Papers*. They should be available in most major research libraries. The PRO holds a set in record class ZHC 1. Included are returns of strengths of units, returns of officers (sometimes even nominal lists) and men, and regulations (covering such matters as organization, pay, training). A complementary set of returns, 1803 to 1815, and indicating the state of readiness achieved on the embodiment of units ordered during the Napoleonic Wars, for both Militia and Volunteers, will be found in HO 50/57-329. Correspondence on various matters concerning the Militia (principally embodiment and regulations) covering the years 1782 to 1840 will be found in HO 50/16-39. In addition, a wide range of matters touching the Militia was considered by the Privy Council. The records are in the Privy Council Registers (PC 2). Militia Returns to the War Office, 1806 to 1830, are in WO 24/612-648.

Some County Returns of the Militia were also submitted to the Privy Council and have been placed in record class PC 1. It is not known why the Privy Council received some Returns but not others. I list those that were included, together with their complete references:

Worcestershire
1789 (PC 1/18, bundle A19)
1790 (PC 1/18, bundle A21)
December 1791 (PC 1/19, bundle A23)
15 January 1794 (PC 1/21, bundle A33)
January and February 1795 (PC 1/24, bundle A43)
January 1799 (PC 1/41, bundle A135)
26 December 1798 (PC 1/37, bundle A148)

Lincolnshire
5 April 1797 (PC 1/37, bundle A115)
7 March 1797 (PC 1/37, bundle A113)
10 March 1797 (PC 1/41, bundle A135)*
2 February 1799 (PC 1/43, bundle A15)
28 March 1809 (PC 1/13/160)

*   A Cavalry Ballot which may have concerned the Militia

Middlesex
1789 (PC 1/18, bundle A19)
1790 (PC 1/18, bundle 21)
January 1792 (PC 1/19, bundle A27)
15 January 1794 (PC 1/21, bundle A33)
January and February 1795 (PC 1/24, bundle A43)

Oxford
February 1798 (PC 1/41, bundle A135)
September 1799 (PC 1/44, bundle A159)

Wigton
May 1798 (PC 1/42, bundle A141)

Cardiganshire
1788 (PC 1/18, bundle A17)

Yorkshire, Durham, Hereford and Northumberland
September 1799 (PC 1/44, bundle A159)

General Militia Returns
August 1796 (PC 1/35, bundle A96)
28 January 1797 (PC 1/37, bundle A112)
1 to 14 February 1797 (PC 1/37, bundle A112)*
3 January 1798 (PC 1/40, bundle A113)
May 1798 (PC 1/42, bundle A141)**

* Contains both Cavalry and Militia returns
** Includes Militia Orders and Schedules

The Royal Warrant for the embodiment of the Supplementary Militia, 1798, is in WO 68/188 (p 1). Indexed records of the arrangements concerning embodiment and disembodiment, 1798 and 1799, are in WO 6/188. Indexed orders as to the embodiment of the Supplementary Militia, 1803, are in WO 1/772, WO 6/190 (p 185), WO 6/191 and WO 6/193 (pp 455-460), and as to the disembodiment of 1802, in WO 6/193 (p

384) and WO 43/31 (p 1). The names of the commanding officers of the English and Scottish units, 1803, are listed in WO 6/176, pp 328-331.

1.1.3 Politics and Police Duties

The formation of a military force, standing apart from the regular army, could not escape a part in the politics of eighteenth and nineteenth century England, particularly those that opposed parliament to the King. The majority of records that belong to those debates are to be found among the private collections left by the major political figures and military officers of the day, and also in general political comment and parliamentary oratory.

Very few, if any, of those records will be found in the Public Record Office.

Contemporary private papers indicate that the county based structure of the Militia was resented by the regular army. However, it was to prove a strong, sentimental binding force and appears to have underlain the army restructuring policy of Cardwell in the 1870s.

Mention has already been made of the police duties of the Irish Militia. In Scotland, on the other hand, it was explicitly stated in 1819 that the Militia was not empowered to assist in the suppression of illicit distillation of spirits and smuggling (WO 43/132). The Suffolk Militia, with a regular army unit, was sent to help the Mayor of Lynn suppress the riots, 27 June 1822, during the Norfolk elections (WO 43/178). A War Office despatch concerning militia police duties is illustrated as **figure 1**.

Correspondence relating to the use of troops, including Militia, to reinforce civil powers, can be found in Home Office General Correspondence in HO 45.

1.1.4 Regimental Movements

Marching orders for the Militia, 1759 to 1820, are in WO 5. The whereabouts of militia units can be determined from the weekly State of the Militia records and Monthly Returns, 1759 to 1925, which are in WO 68. In that same record class are digests of regimental services and regimental histories, together with order books, both general and regimental. It is possible, too, to reconstruct a regiment's movements from information contained in Muster Lists and Pay Books, 1780 to 1878, which are in WO 13.

It should be noted that the date of the embodiment of a regiment is not the date (14 March 1794) given for the appointment of the Colonels (usually holding the rank of Lieutenant Colonel) of the regiments and sometimes of their permanent staff. Embodiment and disembodiment, that is to say the enrolling of men in the regiment and their demobilization, took place when required.

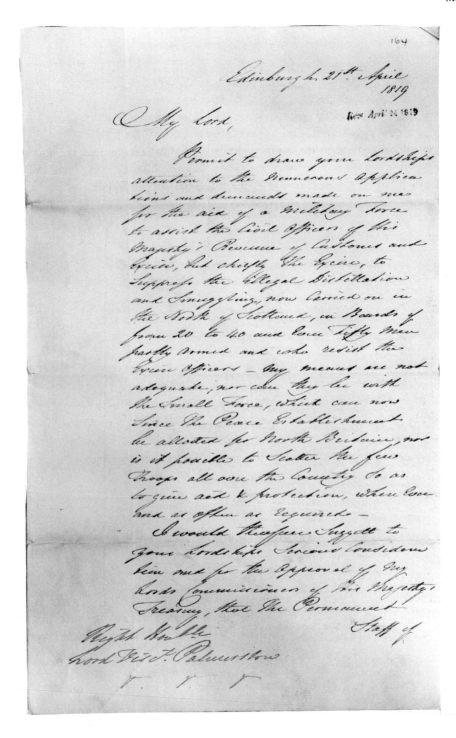

Fig 1. Despatch to Lord Palmerston concerning Militia policing of illicit distillation and smuggling in Scotland, 1819. (WO 43/132 f.164)

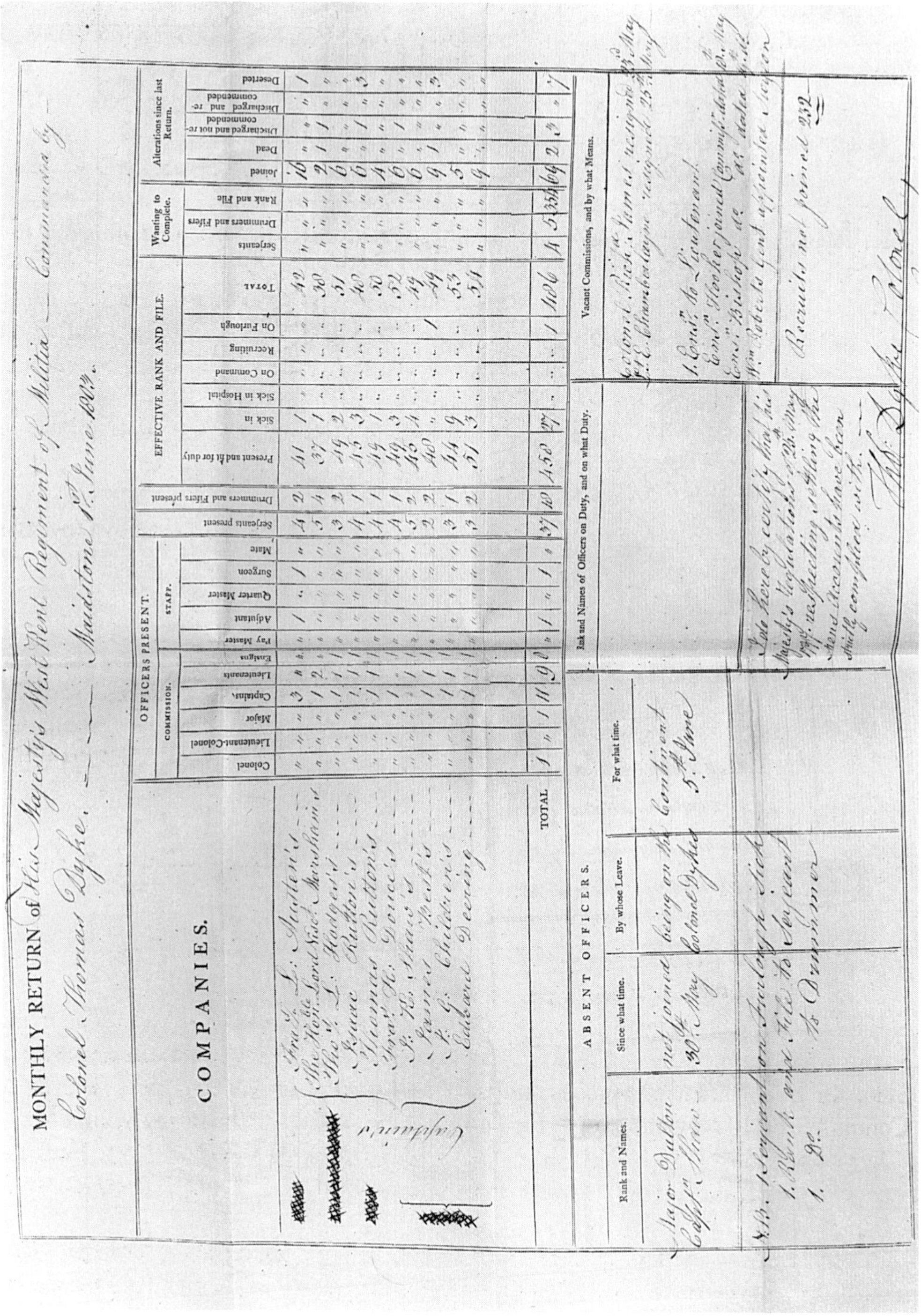

Fig 2. Monthly return of the West Kent Militia, June 1803, including details of appointments and resignations. (WO 17/929, pt 1)

Circulars about camps and the need for uniformity may be found in WO 3/11, 14 and 28. A narrative of the camps may be found in the private papers of Lord Amherst (WO 34/126, 137 and 154). Training seems for the most part to have taken place in the months of February, March and April: for the year 1797 see WO 4/824, papers 50-184. It also seems to have involved a period of 20 days, for which clothing and arms were, pursuant to the Militia Act 1796, ss 25 and 29, supplied (WO 4/828, paper 1). Discussion about punishment for absenteeism from training will be found in a paper of that same year, dated 5 April 1797, in HO 50/28. It was generally considered a good thing that the Militia should train with the regular army (WO 27/40, paper 251). Apparently the camps and training ran smoothly. A month after embodiment 33 units were deemed to be in a reasonable state of readiness (WO 27/40). In 1797 General Dundas could report that most units had been raised and trained (WO 30/65, paper 4). Records concerning the Secretary at War's payments for encampment sites, and concerning refusals of payment, are in WO 4/771. Review Regulations for camps and training are in WO 3/26; in 1779 the Lancashires requested a printed copy (WO 32/157, paper 94).

A sort of 'case study' of the Militia and its activities in 1778 emerges from the War Office correspondence in WO 1/1000.

1.1.5 Tower Hamlets Militia

Because the office of Constable of the Tower of London carried with it command of the Tower Hamlets Militia, records of the regiments are included among the Constable's Office Papers, Official Correspondence and Regulations, 1690 to 1808, in WO 94/67/1. Correspondence about placing the Colours in the Armoury is in WO 94/67/4.

In 1831 the First Regiment of the Tower Hamlets Militia was redesignated the King's Own Light Infantry Militia (WO 43/579).

1.1.6 Channel Islands Militia

Some of the very early records concerning the Channel Islands Militia are to be found among records of the Privy Council. They include the Jersey Militia Laws and Acts of State for Banishment of Persons Refusing to Conform to Militia Laws, referred to Committee on 14 November 1798 (PC 1/43, bundle A148) and the Jersey Militia Act of 7 December 1798 (PC 1/43, bundle A148). A letter dated 5 March 1791, from the Treasury, on the subject of clothing for the Alderney Militia, is in PC 1/19, bundle A23.

A file of the 'Old Series' of the Secretary at War's correspondence, 1840 to 1856, contains records of the Guernsey Militia, a Royal Warrant of 7 September 1843 respecting the enrolment of Chelsea out-pensioners in the Guernsey Militia, together with the printed *Ordonnance de la Cour royale de Guernsey concernant la milice*, 1840 (WO 43/729). In the same series a file, dated 1842-1843, gives details of the establishment and pay of

Channel Islands Militia regiments, and includes a detailed report on the Royal Jersey Militia (WO 43/784). Records relating to the redesignation of Channel Islands Militia, 1927 to 1929, are in WO 32/3638 (under code 57A). More general records of the Channel Islands Militia, concerning such matters as service liability and exemptions, overseas service, embodiment, mobilization, and their relations with the Territorials and transfers to them, 1919 to 1948, are to be found in WO 32 (under code 57A). Additional records of proposals concerning the Jersey and Guernsey Militia, in the years 1945 to 1948, are in DEFE 2/1358.

1.1.7 Militia Chaplains, Quartermasters and Clerks

No provision was made in 1760 for the appointment of Militia Chaplains. However, some references concerning Militia Chaplains from 1797 will be found in Home Office entry books to correspondence with the War Office, in HO 50/128.

Among the 'A and O Papers' of the War Office, paper 968, dated 1884, concerns the 'Old' Militia Quartermasters (WO 33/42). Between 1871 and 1876 the defalcation by a Quartermaster of the Middlesex Militia posed the legal problem whether the adjutant, Captain R McEwen, bore liability for the debt; legal opinion was obtained on the validity of the government bond to cover the debt (WO 43/826).

In 1852 and 1853 the question of payment of Militia Clerks for general and sub-divisional meetings was raised. It was decided that payment was not applicable for voluntary enlistment (WO 43/901).

1.1.8 Billeting and Complaints against the Militia

Dating to 1761 are bound copies of correspondence between Militia colonels and the Secretary at War, concerning the bad behaviour of the Duke of Richmond's Regiment (WO 43/404). Individuals were named in the complaint of the rope-makers and flax-dressers of Lincoln against a militiaman in 1816 (WO 43/116).

A disliked burden on the civil population was, understandably, billeting. Records in the 'Old Series' of the Secretary at War's correspondence document the stratagems employed by innkeepers to avoid it as much as possible. In a file dated 1853-1855 we find that an innkeeper had given money in lieu of lodging to men of Tower Hamlets Militia (WO 43/906). The same file contains a record of increases of daily allowances to householders. Legal opinion of 1843 stated that innkeepers must billet men and horses or provide alternative accommodation for them, and cited the case of Bridge of Alne innkeeper, Alnwick, Northumberland.

1.1.9 Agent General of Militia

The Militia required agents to handle such matters as procurement of supplies and finances. The records of the office of the Agent General of Militia — records for the period 1803 to 1817 are all that have survived — are in WO 7/110-121. Even so, not all years are represented for all departments. The records of the Public Departments, 1809 to 1811, are in WO 7/110; of the regiments, 1813 to 1817, in WO 7/111-112; of Receivers and Treasurers, 1809 to 1816, in WO 7/113-114; of Clerks of Sub-Divisions, 1809 to 1817, in WO 7/115-118; and of Inspecting Officers, 1803 to 1817, in WO 7/119-121.

The 'Declared Accounts' of the Agent General of Militia for the period 1808-1813 can be found in AO 1/280/1042-1048.

1.2 Pay and Accounts

The main collection of Militia regimental pay books is in record class WO 13 (years 1780 to 1878). An example is reproduced as **figure 3**. Other pay books will be found in WO 68 (years 1859 to 1925). Bounties paid to recruits on enlistment were recorded in Bounty Books. The only surviving Bounty Book in the PRO is that for the Cambridge Militia in WO 68/148-149. A sample page is reproduced as **Figure 14**.

In-Letters of the Office of Army Accounts and of the Secretary at War relating to accounts are in the selected 'A' papers in WO 41 (years 1810 to 1822). Amongst other things, they deal with payments to Militia, Yeomanry and Volunteers. That same record class includes registers showing the subject of each paper and its disposal.

Among the records of the Paymaster General's Office are those of the allowances for disembodied Militia, Yeomanry and Volunteers, 1793 to 1927 (PMG 13).

The War Office Accounts in WO 9 include records relating to the Militia. Militia accounts, 1809 to 1818, are in WO 9/13-14. The Journal of Issues of the Militia has not survived in its entirety:

WO 9/15	1760-1761
WO 9/16	1829
WO 9/ 17	1830
WO 9/18	1853-1855

Registers of warrants for the pay of the Militia are in their own idiosyncratic order: WO 9/19 (1795-1803), WO 9/20 (1805-1808), WO 9/21 (1804-1822) and WO 9/22 (1812-1820). The Militia Sub-Divisional Accounts for 1813 (which include records of fines paid in respect of exemption from Militia service) are in WO 9/23. The accounts for the South Hampshire Militia, 1780-1782, are in WO 9/24. WO 9/25 contains circulars and similar papers relating to Militia accounts, 1808 to 1814.

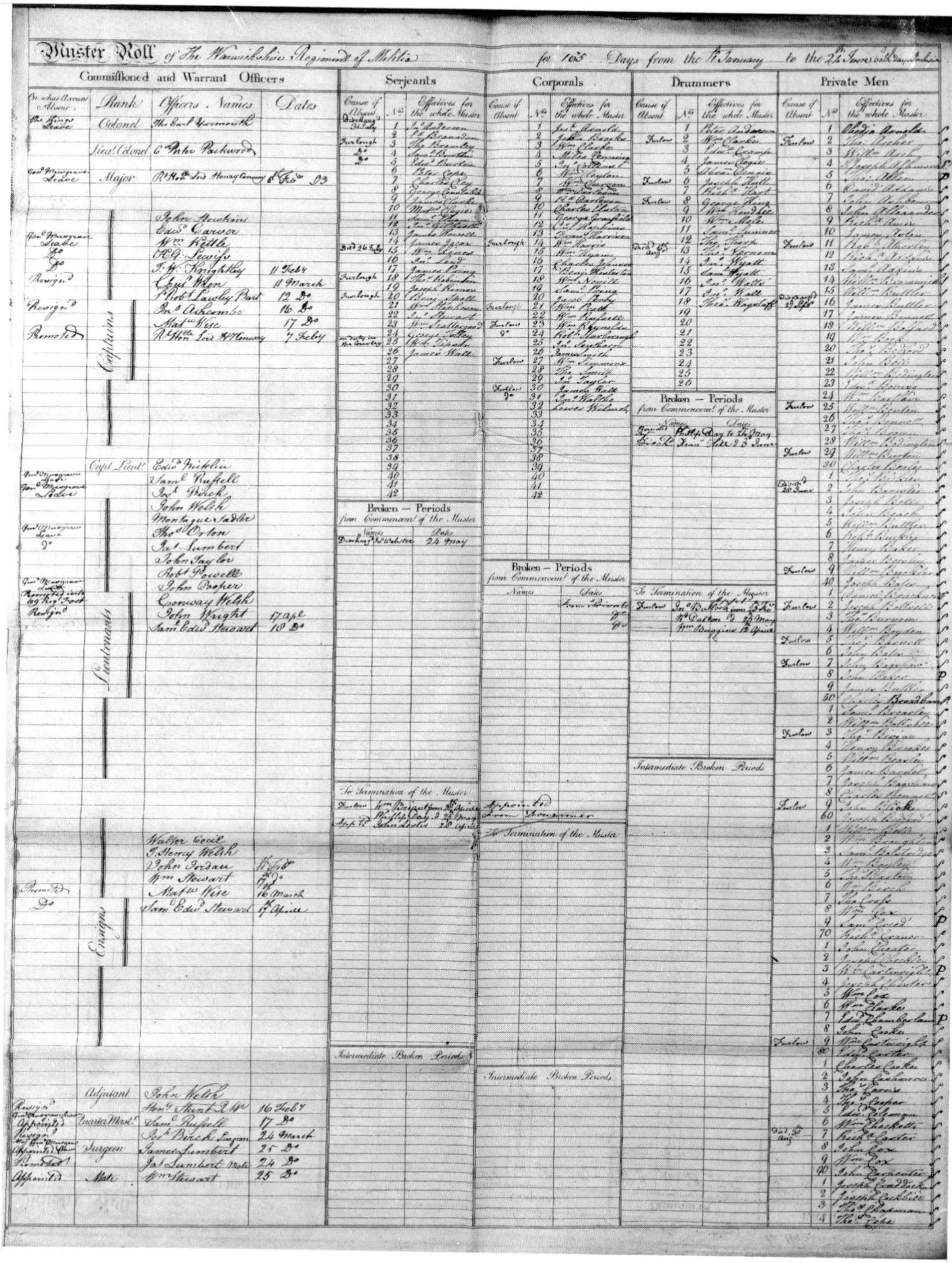

Fig 3. Details from the 1st Warwick Militia pay list, 1794. (WO 13/2194)

Records for the establishment of half pay officers, 1713 to 1824, are in WO 24.

Section 2 of the Militia Act 1803 made provision for the payment, by the parish where the militiamen lived, of an allowance to their families when the men were away from their homes, serving with their regiment. Details relating to this 'Parish Relief', are set out in WO 40/20-21. Details of these allowances and payments sometimes as lump sums rather than as payments to specific named individuals, but sometimes as payments to wives who are named, may be found in E 182, Particulars of Accounts of Land and Assessed Taxes. Various other Militia accounts may be found in this class, including Surgeon's Allowances (payment for medical inspection of new recruits), Marching Guinea Accounts (payment of bounties to new recruits) and Local Militia (expenses for the administration of the local Militia, which can include dates of meetings when the Ballot was discussed).

The class E 182 is arranged by county and then by date and is not listed in detail. Any search for Militia accounts can therefore only be speculative. Except for deserters, for which there is a card index (see section 1.6) there are no indexes by persons name. Further details relating to payment of allowances may be found in parish records, which are not in the custody of the Public Record Office, but normally in diocesan or county record offices.

Among the general series of registers of papers of the War Office are papers relative to the pay and allowances of other ranks of the Reserve Forces, Militia, Yeomanry and Volunteers: emoluments for the Post-War National Service Militia, 1946 to 1950 (WO 32/11987), and Terms and Conditions of Service for Section 'D' of the Royal Army Reserve (WO 32/13626). Records concerning matters of pay and allowances for officers, 1881 to 1946, are in WO 32 (under codes 39G and 39L). In 1853 and 1854 rates of pay for NCOs and men of the Militia Artillery were raised above those in line regiments, eliciting correspondence between the Home Secretary, Viscount Palmerston, and Secretary at War, Sidney Herbert (WO 43/903).

Regulations concerning pay appear regularly among War Office Circulars and Militia Regulations and Letters in WO 123.

In 1828 the Secretary at War issued a directive to Militia staff, to the effect that local tradesmen must not allow militiamen credit limits beyond their pay limit (WO 43/429).

The Militia units, like the line regiments, were dependent upon the services of the regimental agents and bankers. The records of the Agent General for the Militia, 1809 to 1817, are in WO 7/110-121. The indexes to correspondence of the Militia Agents General, 1803 and 1804, are in WO 2. The failure of the Chichester based bank, Ridge and Newlands, 1841-1842, resulted in payment difficulties for the Duke of Richmond's Sussex Militia and the 2nd Dragoons (WO 43/773).

1.3 Service Records

1.3.1 Officers

Brief details of the service career of a militia officer can be gleaned from information contained in the list of *Officers of the Several Regiments and Corps of Militia*, published by the War Office from 1794 onwards (see **Figure 4**), and in the annually published *Army Lists and Militia Lists* which are available on open access shelving in the Microfilm Reading Room and Library. Those publications should also be available in major research libraries. The Office of the Lord Lieutenant of Ireland, Dublin Castle, published in 1810 *A List of Officers of ... Militia ... upon the Establishment of Ireland*. A copy of it is available on open access shelving in the Microfilm Reading Room.

A considerable volume of information concerning the Militia was periodically presented to the House of Commons. Such *Parliamentary Papers* are usually in the form of statistical returns for each unit. Some of them, however, contain names: *Return of the Names of the Colonels and other Officers of the different Regiments of Militia in England and Wales; the Dates of their Commissions; Listing those who have Served in the Royal Household Brigade, the Line or the Royal Navy, 1839* (HC 1839, xxxi, 267: PRO reference ZHC 1/1260). A similar return was published the year following, but listing certain regiments only (HC 1840, xxx, 253: PRO reference ZHC 1/1309). It was some years before the next such list was published: *Nominal Return of Officers holding Commissions in Militia and in Volunteer Corps* (HC 1862, xxxii, 583: PRO reference ZHC 1/2816). *The London Calendar, or Court and City Register* (London, 1782-1812) contains, *inter alia*, lists of Militia Officers. Commissions were gazetted in the *London Gazette*, a publication held in major research libraries, and also at the PRO in record class ZJ 1.

Until the middle years of the nineteenth century, the Militia was the responsibility of the Home Office, and early records of Militia officers' service are to be found in Home Office archives. In the military correspondence of the Home Office, 1780 to 1840 (HO 50), are lists of commissions into the Militia and the Volunteers, together with returns of service. The Military Entry Books of the Home Office, 1758 to 1855 (HO 51), include records of commissions, appointments and warrants for Militia officers, some of which records overlap with the register of commissions in WO 4/9. Sixty-seven original officers' Commissions, mostly on parchment, belonging to the years 1780 to 1874, are in WO 43/1059. Militia commissions were not liable to stamp duty, according to legal opinion of the years 1852 to 1854; but the Secretary at War advised that 'some remuneration' should be made to the Lord Lieutenant's clerks for their preparation (WO 43/883).

Some records of Militia officers' service are to be found among the general records of regular army officers' service in WO 76 (see Appendix 3 for a full list of Militia officers

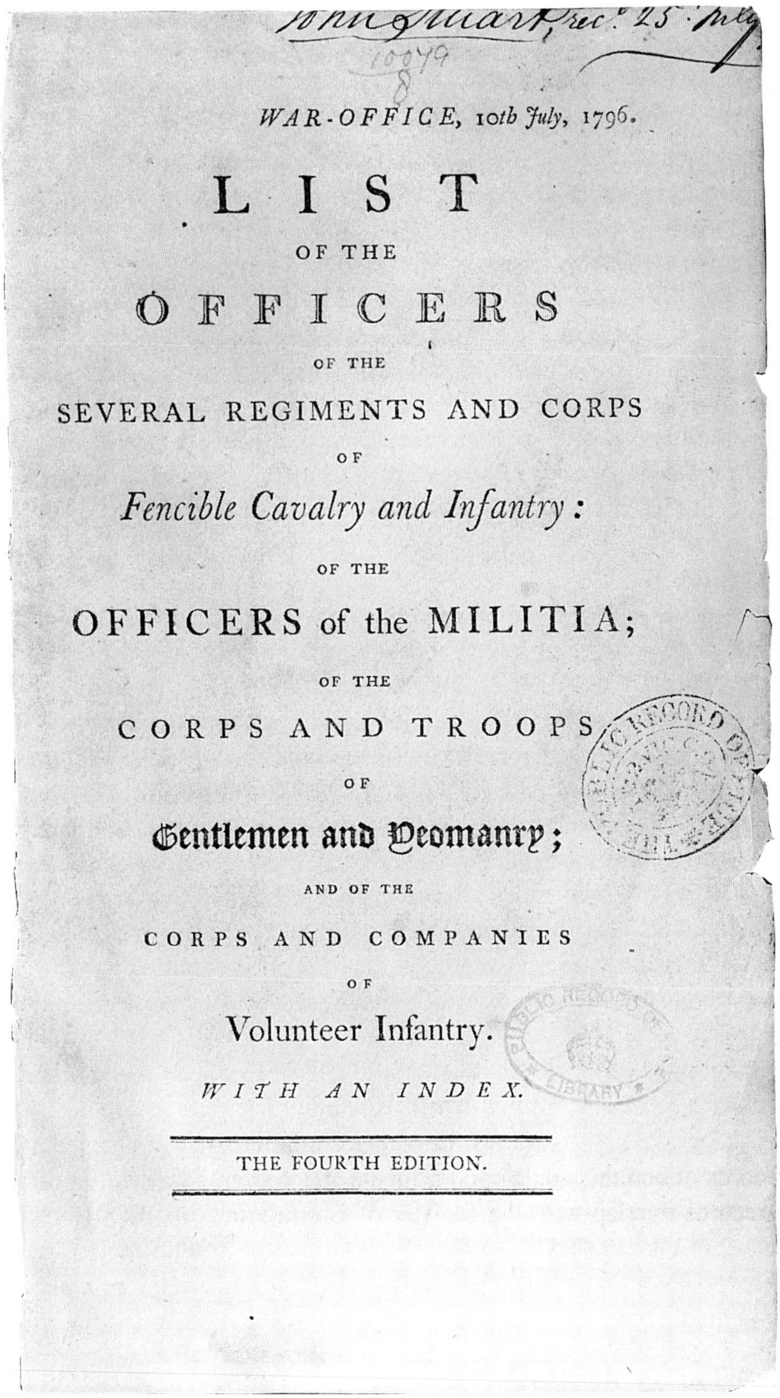

John Stuart, rec.d 25 July
10049
8

WAR-OFFICE, 10th *July*, 1796.

LIST

OF THE

OFFICERS

OF THE

SEVERAL REGIMENTS AND CORPS

O F

Fencible Cavalry and Infantry:

OF THE

OFFICERS of the MILITIA;

OF THE

CORPS AND TROOPS

O F

𝕲𝖊𝖓𝖙𝖑𝖊𝖒𝖊𝖓 𝖆𝖓𝖉 𝖄𝖊𝖔𝖒𝖆𝖓𝖗𝖞;

AND OF THE

CORPS AND COMPANIES

O F

Volunteer Infantry.

WITH AN INDEX.

_____

THE FOURTH EDITION.

_____

Fig 4. The title page from the War Office's published 1796 Militia List, giving the names of all officers of the Militia and the units in which they served.

records in WO 76). References to officers appear in various registers of the Militia, 1816 to 1824, in WO 25, and in the Muster Rolls and Pay Lists, 1780 to 1878, in WO 10. Among various private collections of papers presented to the War Office between the World Wars, and thereupon deposited in the Public Record Office in WO 79, are original records of commissions of some Militia regiments, together with lists of officers and other records of officers' service. Commission Books for the Irish Militia, 1794, are in WO 25/118.

References to Militia officers figure, also, among records of the various military establishments, eg half pay, 1713 to 1824, and compassionate list, 1779 to 1812, in WO 24.

In 1780 legal opinions and correspondence on the holding of army rank by Militia officers were collected, together with letters of Charles Jenkinson to the Judge Advocate General, Sir Charles Gould (WO 43/403).

1.3.2 Other Ranks

Of prime value as sources of information about a militiaman's service career are the Attestation Papers, 1806 to 1915, in WO 96 (see **Figure 15**). Attestations are the loose forms that were filled in by the recruit on enlistment and that, in most cases, were annotated throughout his career up to the date of his discharge, so that they constitute effectively a record of his service. Date and place of birth are stated as well. The basic arrangement of records within WO 96 is according to regiment in order of seniority; thereunder, the forms are arranged in alphabetical order of militiaman's surname. The Attestation Papers of Local Militia Regiments, 1769 to 1854, arranged in alphabetical order of militiaman's surname, are in WO 97/1091-1112 (see **Figure 5**). A computerized name index of these records is available in the Microfilm Reading Room. Such papers were preserved only in the case of militiamen discharged to pension.

The Pensions Registers of the Royal Hospital Chelsea provide some biographical and service information about militiamen pensioners. The registers of Militia pensions, 1821 to 1829 (WO 23), provide the following information: name, age, length of service, cause of discharge and date of death. The information provided in the Admission Books of Chelsea Hospital (WO 116 and WO 117) includes a brief description of the militiaman, his age, place of birth, particulars of service and reason for discharge. Entries in both sets of registers are arranged according to the date of meeting of the Pension Board.

In the absence of such records, biographical information about a militiaman can be sometimes found in the Musters and Pay Books of Militia regiments, 1780 to 1878 in WO 13 - see section 1.2. Moreover, such documents are interesting in their own right, insofar as they provide background information about the regiment's location, expenses and miscellaneous payments. Additional pay lists and other nominal rolls of militiamen will be found among the Militia records, 1759 to 1925, in WO 68.

WO 68 contains also the surviving Enrolment Books which, provided that they were fully filled in at the time, should contain the following information: name, size at enlistment and at 24 years of age, physical description, place of birth (county, city or town, together with parish), place and date of attestation, period of service, former service (and whether entitled to pension from previous military service), promotions, casualties (whether deserted, discharged, transferred or dead) and observations.

The Casualty Books, also in WO 68, the primary function of which was to list desertions, discharges, transfers and deaths of militiamen, often also contain information about marriages and births of children.

The Militia Reserve originated in the 1880s, and provided the regular army with a pool of militiamen who were specially attested for General Service, ie with the Regular Forces overseas in time of war (though subject to certain mitigating conditions). Attestations are in both WO 96 and WO 97.

1.4 Medals

Prior to the South African or Boer War (1899-1902), no campaign medals are known to have been awarded to militiamen as militiamen, and no Militia medal roll is in the custody of the Public Record Office. It follows that a man known to have been a militiaman and to have been awarded a medal will have gained that award in some other branch of the armed forces, the records of which should be searched. In general, militiamen did not serve overseas, and their service was often for comparatively short periods of time, facts which would in any event reduce the occasions upon which a militiaman might have gained such an award. Nevertheless, during the opening years of the twentieth century (1901 to 1904), discussion concerning a Militia Long Service Medal and a proposal to institute a new Auxiliary Forces Order generated files now in WO 32/5992, 7245-7247. Records of the subsequent award of Militia Long Service and Good Conduct Medals are in WO 102/22.

Militia battalions took part in the South African War as regular components of their respective regiments and, consequently, militiamen became eligible for the award of the Queen's South Africa Medal (QSA) and of the King's South Africa Medal (KSA) with bars. Records are in WO 100.

During the South African War a Queen's Mediterranean Medal (1899-1902) was instituted. The medal, for which no bars were awarded, is exactly the same as the Queen's South Africa Medal except that the word 'Mediterranean' appears on the reverse

HIS MAJESTY'S

Warwickshire REGT. OF *Militia*

Whereof *The Right Honble The Earl of Warwick* is Colonel.

These are to Certify,

I.
Age and Enlistment.
THAT *John Petty Serjeant* born in the Parish of *Chilvers Coton* in or near the Town of *Nuneaton* in the County of *Warwick* was enlisted for the aforesaid Regiment at *Coleshill* in the County of *Warwick* on the 13th Day of *October* at the Age of *Twenty two* for

II.
Service.
THAT he hath served in the Army for the space of *Forty Years* Years and *Two hundred & Thirty* Days, after the Age of Eighteen, according to the subjoined

STATEMENT OF SERVICE.

IN WHAT CORPS.	PERIOD OF SERVICE.		Serjeant Major.		Qr. Mast. Serjeant.		Serjeant.		Corporal.		Trumpeter or Drummer.		Private.		Serving prior to the Age of Eighteen to be deducted.		Total Service.	
	From	To	Yrs.	Days	Yrs.	Days	Yrs.	Days	Yrs.	Days	Yrs.	Days	Yrs.	Days	Yrs.	Days	Yrs.	Days
Warwick Militia	13th Octr 1790	31st May 1831					33	37	2	121			5	72			40	230
Total of Service							33	37	2	121			5	72			40	230
In East or W. Indies																		

III.
Authority and Cause of Discharge.
THAT by Authority of *Colonel The Earl of Warwick* dated
HE IS HEREBY DISCHARGED in consequence of *Age and Infirmity*

IV.
Not disqualified for Pension.
THAT he is not to my knowledge, incapacitated by the Sentence of a General Court Martial, from receiving Pension.

V.
Character, &c. &c. &c.
THAT his general Conduct as a Soldier has been *Very good*

VI.
Settlement of all Demands.
THAT he has received all just Demands of Pay, Clothing, &c., from his Entry into the Service to the date of this Discharge, as appears by his Receipt underneath.

VII.
Acknowledgment of the Receipt of all Demands.
I *John Petty Serjt.* do hereby acknowledge that I have received all my Clothing, Pay, Arrears of Pay, and all just Demands whatsoever, from the time of my Entry into the Service to the time of this Discharge.

Certified by *John Brookman Adjt* Commanding the Troop or Company.

Signature of the Soldier. *John P Petty Serjt*

VIII.
Description &c. &c. &c.
To prevent any improper use being made of this Discharge, by its falling into other Hands, the following is a Description of the said *John Petty*
He is about *Sixty two* Years of Age, is *Five* Feet *Ten* Inches in height, *Grey* Hair, *Dark* Eyes *Dark* Complexion, and by Trade or Occupation a *Weaver*

Given under my Hand, and the Seal of the Regiment, at *Warwick* this 21st Day of *June* 1831.

Signature of the Commanding Officer *Warwick, Col*

Horse-Guards, _____ 18 , confirmed _____

Fig 5. The discharge document of John Petty, 1st Warwick Militia, 1831. (WO 97/ 1106)

and that the words 'South Africa' were deleted. It was awarded to the third or Militia battalions of the following regiments: Royal Northumberland Fusiliers, Royal Fusiliers, West Yorkshire, Loyal North Lancashire, Royal West Kent, King's Own Yorkshire Light Infantry, Seaforth Highlanders and Royal Munster Fusiliers. The overseas service in respect of which the medal was awarded was for garrison duty in the Mediterranean (Malta), guarding South African prisoners of war. The medal roll is in WO 100/368, and references can be found on Attestations in WO 96.

The Militia Reserve, who were specially attested for General Service with the Regular Army overseas in time of war, were treated as regular soldiers entitled to the QSA and KSA with bars (WO 100).

1.5 Casualties

Lists of casualties among militiamen, 1759 to 1925, figure among Militia records in WO 68. For the period of the South African War, records of casualties of men of the Special Reserve (that is, the militiamen attested for service with the Imperial Yeomanry) may be found among the Casualty Books in WO 129/8-11, and in the Lists of Casualties, October 1899 to August 1902, in WO 108/338 (formerly WO 108/83).

1.6 Deserters

References to deserters may sometimes be found in regimental Muster Lists and Pay Books (WO 13). References to deserters for whose apprehension a reward was paid by local tax officials may be found amongst the subsidiary documents of the Receivers' Accounts of Land and Assessed Taxes (E 182), arranged by county and date. A nominal card index thereto is also available in the Research Enquiries Room in index card drawers 50-73. The counties covered by this index are Bedfordshire, Berkshire, Buckinghamshire, Cambridgeshire, Cheshire and Middlesex. A list of Militia deserters, 1811 to 1820, is to be found in WO 25/2934, where in many cases a full personal description is given in addition to details of age, place of birth, date of enlistment, place and date of desertion and how disposed of. Other references to deserters are to be found among the general registers of military deserters in WO 25/2906 and following, and for the years 1744 to 1858 in WO 4/591-654. In July 1799 a proclamation was drafted for the pardoning of deserters from the Militia. A copy together with a report from the Attorney General is in PC 1/44, bundle A156.

1.7 Courts Martial

Surviving records of Militia courts martial are in WO 68. Records of Militia courts martial may also be found among the papers of the Judge Advocate General's Office in WO 71.

1.8 Pensions

The Royal Hospital Chelsea, founded in 1681 as a permanent hospital for the care of disabled soldiers, admitted its first pensioner in 1692. Along with Kilmainham Hospital in Dublin, which had been in existence for the same purpose since 1679, these hospitals cared for those soldiers from both the regular army and the Militia who need help after they had left the service. From 1822, when there were too many in pensioners for the space available in the hospitals, both in and out pensions (for those men who lived away from Chelsea or Kilmainham) were administered by Chelsea.

1.8.1 Militiamen

Records of pensions and allowances for militiamen, 1817 to 1927, and for Volunteers and Yeomanry for some of those years, are in PMG 13/4-50.

There are lists of militiamen eligible for pension up to 1830 among the Subsidiary Documents to the Receivers' Accounts (E 182) - see section 1.2. The arrangement of those accounts is by county and date. There is no general, nominal index.

Among the Chelsea Hospital pension registers is the Militia Class Book, Christmas 1806 to June 1807 (WO 23/140, ff 1-52). It lists the regiment, the militiaman's name, his age in years, length of service (in years, but sometimes also with indication of months), station (ie rank) in the army, admission date (ie to pension, otherwise date of discharge from the Militia), complaint (ie basis of discharge from the Militia), residence (town and county, not street) and date of muster, either 11, 12 or 26 December 1806. Registers of out-pensioners of Chelsea Hospital, covering militiamen discharged to pension on the ground of disability up to 1913, are in WO 116. The entries are arranged in chronological order of meetings of the Pension Board. In addition, there is a list of pensioners discharged from Militia and Yeomanry regiments, 1821 to 1829, in WO 23/25, where date of death is also indicated; and there are registers of pension payments to disembodied Militia, Yeomanry, Local Militia and Volunteer Corps, 1868 to 1882, in WO 23/89-91. A register of payment of Auxiliary Forces' pensions, 1882 to 1892, is to be found in WO 23/92. Warrants granting pensions to Militia Sergeants are listed in the House of Commons Papers for 1823 (HC 1823, xiii, 63: PRO reference ZHC 1/772).

Among the 'Very Old Series' of the Secretary at War's correspondence are records concerning Militia pensions. For the years 1820 to 1822, there are draft warrants to enable reduced adjutants (NCOs) of local Militia to draw allowances as well as their Chelsea and Kilmainham pensions (WO 43/161). Additional records of this type, 1820 to 1823, and legal advice about them, together with a case, are in WO 43/162. And in WO 43/163 are yet more such records for the year 1820, together with draft affidavits, and records of the half pay establishment, 1817 to 1819. In 1823 the Secretary at War received a Memorial from twelve Militia Regimental Paymasters, who are named, seeking improved retirement terms. The same file contains a letter from Paymaster David Stockford, Oxfordshire Militia, dated 1826 (WO 43/316).

Between 1830 and 1832 an acrimonious exchange of notes took place between the Audit Office and the Secretary at War. The Audit Office required information about half pay and retired pay officers of the British Militia and foreign officers holding civil appointments. The Secretary at War repudiated the claim of the Auditors to question payments sanctioned by him (WO 43/555).

Although not pensioners, it is convenient to mention here that in corporate towns in Scotland, ex-militiamen (named) were, between 1818 and 1824, accorded trading privileges (WO 43/110, 164, 165, 167, 169-171). Two other files of this same 'Very Old Series', both dated 1820, of the Secretary at War's office, dealt with the trading privileges of discharged soldiers and local militiamen in corporate towns, including the case of Stephen Meeks, flesher of Haddington (WO 43/141), and the refusal of 'begging protection' to Charles Spottiswood, pedlar of Peebles (WO 43/142).

1.8.2 Families

Lists of wives and children of militiamen who were eligible for pensions are sometimes to be found among the Subsidiary Documents to Receivers' Accounts (E 182). The arrangement is by county and then by date. There is no general, nominal list. Similar lists for Scotland are in the custody of the Scottish Record Office among Lieutenancy and Militia records. A record of payments to wives and children in Midlothian, 1803 to 1815, is in the Exchequer records (SRO reference E. 327/147-158). A file dated 1827-1854 contains persistent claims by Militia adjutants for entitlement of their wives to pensions, together with legal opinion (WO 43/450). By 1855-1856 it had been decided that widows of Militia officers were not entitled to pensions: the decision was applied in the case of Surgeon William T Molloy, Northampton Regiment, who died of illness in Gibraltar (WO 43/917).

Between 1829 and 1833 a file was maintained, in the Secretary at War's office, of letters from the author and travel writer George Borrow of Willow Lane, Norwich, respecting the disembodied Militia allowance made to his brother, Lieutenant John Borrow, West Norfolk Militia, who departed for Mexico leaving two illegitimate children a charge on the parish (WO 43/516).

A nominal list of widows of Militia officers in receipt of pension, 1713 to 1829, is in WO 24.

1.9 Families of Militiamen

Registers of marriages of militiamen and of the births and baptisms of their children, 1759 to 1925, are in WO 68. Certificates of birth and baptism of children of Militia officers, 1793 to 1886, are in WO 32/8903, 8904, 8906-8913, nominal indexes to which are to be found on the open access shelving in the Research Enquiries Room.

References to next of kin sometimes appear on Attestations (WO 96 and WO 97).

2. VOLUNTEERS (1794-1813)

The Volunteers were first raised as an auxiliary military force in 1794. Service was entirely voluntary. Volunteers were not liable to serve outside the Kingdom; but, in time of crisis, provision was made for units to volunteer for service abroad and for individual members to transfer to the Regular Army. In 1799 the Volunteers and other armed associations offered their services for the defence of the country, the record of which is in WO 40/12. Command was vested in the Lord Lieutenant of the county who, in turn, was responsible in this regard, until 1856, to the Home Office. In the military correspondence of the Home Office is to be found correspondence concerning Volunteers, 1797 to 1803 (HO 50/40-56), 1803 to 1853 (HO 51/74-99) and supplementary correspondence, 1794 to 1813 (HO 50/330-356). Other early records, for 1803, are in HO 50/57-312, and a set of the Acts in force relating to the Volunteers, 1799 to 1804, is in HO 51/107. An interesting illustration of local involvement in volunteering is provided by the action of the inhabitants of Hartlepool who, in 1796, formed themselves into Volunteers for the Service of the Coast Batteries (WO 40/8, bundle 22). As a result of the formation, in 1808, of the Local Militia (as distinct from the Militia), based also on limited, voluntary service, the Volunteer Movement dwindled and was dissolved in 1813. The Local Militia was itself dissolved in 1816. The Volunteer Force was revived in 1859.

Surviving records of the Volunteers are mainly to be found in WO 13/4160-4621, but give a far from complete coverage, either in terms of regimental books or in years. A special case is provided by the records of the Royal Preston Volunteers (WO 79/2), which comprise the Minute Books of the Committee of Management, 1797 and 1798; 'Strength Returns' by companies, 1 March 1799; and correspondence for the years 1799 and 1814. They were in private hands until presented to the War Office in March 1939, whence they were deposited in the Public Record Office in WO 79, a record class composed of private collections.

Information about officers appears in the *Army Lists*. Registers of their commissions, 1798 to 1825, are in HO 51/59-73. Their commissions were gazetted in the *London Gazette* (held in major research libraries and by the PRO under reference ZJ 1).

The Establishment Books of the Volunteer Corps, 1802 to 1808, are in HO 51/108-110. Volunteer records for 1804 are in WO 40/21. Increases in the establishment of Yeomanry and Volunteer Corps and the pay and allowances of the newly raised units were documented in 1803 and 1804, and the records together with the Royal Warrant of 22 May 1804 are in WO 43/399. In 1826 the Home Office, at the request of the Secretary at War, submitted a list of the Volunteer Corps of Infantry still existing at 13 May 1826 (WO 43/259).

Fig 6. An 1859 *Punch* cartoon expressing confidence in the ability of the newly raised Rifle Volunteers to repel foreign invasion.

3. RIFLE VOLUNTEERS (1859-1908)

3.1 General and Service Records

The institution in 1859 of the Volunteer Force was a further response to contemporary perception of foreign menace (see **Figure 6**). The units were raised pursuant to a provision of the Yeomanry Act 1804, which until 1863 remained the Act under which Volunteers could be raised. They were at first independent and lacking in co-ordination. In 1860 they were brought together into Administrative Battalions, which in 1881 became Volunteer Battalions of line regiments. The financial state and internal organization of the Volunteer Force was the subject of a memorandum in 1870 (WO 32/21A and 21B, p 426). Other records concerning the organization, manning, formation and disbandment of units and also the transfer to the Territorial Force are in WO 32 (under code 14F). The Volunteer Force ceased to exist in 1908, when most of the battalions became part of the Territorial Force.

The monarch's signed appointments to volunteer units, 1914 to 1918, are in WO 103/31.

The Regulations for the Volunteer Force. War Office, 1881 (London, 1881) list various returns that were to be made by Volunteer units, such as returns at inspection by the local District General Officer Commanding, quarterly returns, and regular submission of copies of the Adjutant's diary of instructions given to the corps. Annual returns were to be made on 1 November by the Officer Commanding, together with a nominal roll; and after both documents had been checked at the War Office, the nominal roll was sent to the Clerk of the Lieutenancy 'to be retained for the information of the Lord Lieutenant'. There was no stipulation regarding regimental books as such, apart from the Adjutant's muster book, a record of attendance at drill and diary, which he was to hand on to his successor. In addition to his other duties, the Adjutant had financial responsibility, but no details of his account books are given, except that they were to be handed over to his successor.

The *Regulations* contain no instruction for the permanent preservation of the books and no obligation was placed upon units to keep them. The early independence of the units left decisions on the fate of the books in the hands of the commanding officers. As a result, regimental books are to be found in a variety of places. Some were placed in regimental museums, others were taken home by the officers and incorporated into their private papers, and some were sold or otherwise disposed of and ultimately reached a variety of museums and record repositories. It is clear, however, that the vast bulk of them have been lost. The returns to the War Office have fared little better. The annual returns that were passed to the Clerk of the Lieutenancy should be amongst the Lieutenancy records in county record offices, but are apparently not. The nominal rolls, the Adjutant's diary and pay lists, held by the War Office, have vanished. All that

Fig 7. Officers and men of the 1st Battalion North Staffordshire Rifle Volunteers, 1863. (COPY 1/5)

seems to have survived is an incomplete set of pay lists for Volunteer Staff, 1873 to 1878, in WO 13/4622-4675, and the regimental books of the 10th Battalion, The London Regiment (known as The Paddington Rifles). The unit was raised in 1860 as the 36th Middlesex Rifle Volunteers, was renumbered as the 18th in 1880, became a battalion of the London Regiment in 1908, and was disbanded in 1912. Those records were passed to the War Office and then transferred to the Public Record Office (WO 70/1-21, where they are incorrectly described), and constitute the only set of Volunteer records in official custody. The record of the formation of another regiment, The Victoria Rifles, of the Middlesex Rifle Volunteers, is in WO 43/843.

Officers and men of the 1 Battalion North Staffordshire Rifle Volunteers in 1863 can be seen in **Figure 7**.

References to officers appear in the *Army Lists*, where the addresses and other brief details of the local units are given. Among *Parliamentary Papers, 1863*, was published a *Nominal Return of Officers holding Commissions in Militia and in Volunteer Corps* (HC 1863, xxxii, 583: PRO reference ZHC 1/2816). A nominal list, not held by the Public Record Office, was published by H E Harris, *The Alphabetical Volunteer List, Containing the Names of the Officers of the Volunteer Force in Great Britain* (Brighton, 1875).

The Scottish Record Office holds a few records of Volunteer Corps: lists of the Dundee Volunteer Rifle Corps in 1859 (SRO reference MD. 7/1), and a muster roll of the 5th Forfarthshire Volunteer Corps, 1859 to 1886 (SRO reference MD. 7/1).

Despite the loss of Volunteer records, it is usually possible to reconstruct, in outline, the history of many units from the very extensive reports in the contemporary local press. Such newspapers are not held by the Public Record Office, but may be accessible locally or at the Newspaper Section of the British Library at Colindale.

3.2 Medals and Awards

The Volunteer Officers' Decoration was instituted in July 1892, to reward efficient and capable officers of the Volunteer Force, and who had given twenty years' service. Records of its institution, 1892 to 1897, are in WO 32 (under code 50W). The registers, 1892 to 1932, are in WO 330/3-4. The registers of awards of the Volunteers' Long Service Medal made to other ranks, 1906 to 1925, are in WO 102/21.

4. FENCIBLE CORPS

The raising of Fencible Corps was yet another means whereby the Government sought to provide for home defence in periods of extreme danger. Unlike the Militia, Fencible Corps did not involve a continuous service liability. Instead, they were raised only at times when the regular army, or the major part of it, was serving overseas. Service liability was restricted to the Kingdom, but Fencible Corps could volunteer to extend their services abroad. A list of Fencible Corps raised for service in Great Britain and Ireland in 1808 and including those who volunteered for overseas service is in WO 40/25 (bundle 20). Service was voluntary but remunerated: Fencibles received a bounty of 3 guineas and pay and allowances as for the regular army.

Surviving Muster Rolls and Pay Lists for the Fencible Cavalry are in WO 13/3726-3785 and for the Fencible Provisional Cavalry in WO 13/3786-3791. They belong to the period 1794 to 1802. The Muster Lists and Pay Books of a mere handful of Fencible regiments, but notably the Isle of Man Fencibles, are in WO 12 (1st Manx Fencibles, 1783 to 1811, in WO 12/10898; 2nd Manx Fencibles, 1796 to 1802, in WO 12/10908; Surrey Fencibles, 1801 to 1802, in WO 12/11093). Records of a disbanding of the 1st Manx Fencibles in 1803 are in WO 40/18, while the records of the Corps of Fencible Infantry for service in the Isle of Man for the same year are in WO 40/19. Other records of Fencible units, including nominal lists, are to be found in the Out-letters of the War Office in WO 4, to which the index is in WO 2/1. A list of Fencible Cavalry units dated 26 May 1796 is contained in a letter on the subject of clothing (WO 4/165, pp 39-40).

The Sea Fencibles were a coastal defence force, recruited from among fishermen and boatmen, under naval command, and to be mobilized in the event of invasion or emergency. The pay lists, 1798 to 1810, are in ADM 28. They consist simply of names of men acknowledging receipt of pay, submitted by officers as vouchers for money expended. They are arranged under district and date.

There is an index to letters from named captains of Irish Sea Fencible and Signal Stations to Army officers, 1808 to 1853, in WO 25/248. It is uncertain where surviving letters are to be found, possibly in War Office In-letters or Admiralty Out-letters (ADM 2). However, a very brief digest of the letters is given in this index.

At the request of the House of Commons, a Return was compiled by the Admiralty, showing by district, the number of men serving in the Sea Fencibles. The Return, dated 9 June 1858, is in ADM 1/5704 (Accountant General paper 645).

It appears that the majority of records concerning the Fencibles have not survived, although some may still be in collections of private papers or deposited in county record offices.

Surviving records concerning the Fencible Irish Militia, 1799 to 1815, are in WO 1/77-778.

5. YEOMANRY (1804-1921)

The Yeomanry, like the Rifle Volunteers, were raised under provisions of the Volunteer Act 1804 until 1921, with a modification introduced by the Militia and Yeomanry Act 1901. They were mounted volunteers, their units formed on a county basis and, until the South African War, liable only for home service. See chapter 6 for details about the Imperial Yeomanry.

Records of the increase in the establishment of the Yeomanry and Volunteer Corps during 1803 and 1804, together with their pay and allowances and the Royal Warrant of 22 May 1804, are to be found in WO 43/399. In 1838, however, the Yeomanry Cavalry underwent a reduction. The records of this, together with a schedule of the regiments, are in WO 43/694. The question of precedence among Yeomanry Cavalry units occupied attention during 1884 and 1885 (WO 32/7238 (under code 6B)). Yeomanry records for the period 1876 to 1942, on a variety of matters, but principally dealing with the transfer of the Yeomanry to the Territorials, are to be found in WO 32 (under code 6B): other matters recorded there concern the state of the Yeomanry, formation of units, terms and conditions of service. The conversion of Yeomanry regiments, 1941 and 1942, is recorded in WO 32/10301 (under code 6B).

Between 1833 and 1835 the Irish Yeomanry Corps were reorganized, and the posts of permanent sergeants and drummers were abolished (WO 43/618).

Regulations for the Yeomanry Cavalry, 1832 and 1833, London: War Office, together with the *Abstract of the Regulations, 1821*, London: War Office, are in WO 43/349. *The Yeomanry Regulations: being an abridgement of the Regulations for the Formations and Movements of the Cavalry, adapted to the use of Yeomanry Corps, 1851* (London, 1853) list a number of forms that were to be returned to the Home Office, and after 1855 to the War Office, by the commanding officers. They were chiefly concerned with the payment of the men during the annual training camps and with the supply of arms and equipment. There was no reference to regimental books before the *Regulations for the Yeomanry Cavalry, War Office, 1894* (London, 1894) required each unit to have an Adjutant's diary, musketry register, squadron return books, returns of target practice and equipment's ledger, which were to be produced as required by inspecting officers, and copies to be submitted regularly. The Adjutant was responsible for paying the unit's permanent staff, though there was no mention of pay books.

There was no regulation for the permanent preservation of Yeomanry books. Their preservation is, in general, bad; the best are in regimental custody, others have been noted in drill halls and in private collections. The only returns known to be in the Public Record Office are some Muster Rolls and Pay Lists of 1803 to 1853, in WO 13/3968 - 4159.

Yeomanry warrants, 1825 to 1852, are in HO 51/100-102. Letters received by the Home Office from Yeomanry and Volunteers, 1802 and 1803, are in HO 51/103. Registers of Returns for Yeomanry and associated corps, 1794 to 1803, and an index to those returns are in HO 51/104-106. Yeomanry accounts ledgers, 1831 to 1839, are in WO 9/47.

The abolition of the post of Brigade Major in the Irish Yeomanry between 1830 and 1834 led to letters and memorials from redundant officers (named) seeking retirement pay (WO 43/351).

In the English and Scottish Yeomanry Cavalry returns of 1827, certain regiments were named with their complements: Herefordshire, North Somerset, Wiltshire, Royal Linlithgowshire, Renfrewshire, Roxburghshire and Louth (WO 43/223).

Records concerning pensions of adjutants and sergeants of disbanded regiments of Yeomanry Cavalry, 1827 and 1828, are in WO 43/419.

A volume containing details of the service of officers of the Northampton Yeomanry between 1874 and 1912 can be found in WO 76/14.

Details relating to the award of the Territorial Decoration and the Territorial Efficiency Medal and Territorial Force Efficiency Medal, to which members of the Yeomanry were eligible after 1908, can be found in chapter 7.

Operational records and records of service for the First World War are covered in chapter 8.

6. THE IMPERIAL YEOMANRY (1899-1902)

6.1 Introduction

The Imperial Yeomanry was formed in late 1899 as a direct result of the need for mounted infantry in South Africa. Unlike the conventional yeomanry, which only saw service at home, the Imperial Yeomanry was recruited for service overseas. Details relating to the formation of the Imperial Yeomanry can be found in WO 32/7866.

6.2 General Records

The majority of records relating to the formation and administration of the Imperial Yeomanry can be found amongst the records in WO 108, South African War Papers. WO 108/194-228, 375 and 395 deal exclusively with the Imperial Yeomanry. WO 108/212-221 contain details relating to the commissioning of officers. WO 108/395 contains Imperial Yeomanry Orders, 1900-1903, in which can be found details about commissions, promotions and casualties.

The records of Brigadier General R B Colvin, Officer Commanding 20 Battalion, Imperial Yeomanry, can be found in WO 136.

6.3 Service Records

6.3.1 Other Ranks

The attestation and discharge papers of those men who served in the Imperial Yeomanry are in the class WO 128. These papers are almost identical to the regular army and Militia attestation and discharge papers in WO 97 and WO 96 respectively, and contain similar types of information (see **Figure 9**).

The records in WO 128 are arranged in Imperial Yeomanry service number order. In order to find the service number of an individual who served in the Imperial Yeomanry you need to consult the registers of service numbers in the class WO 129. The registers in WO 129 each cover a range of service numbers.

WO 129/1	IY Service No 1-7299
WO 129/2	IY Service No 7300-19999
WO 129/3	IY Service No 20000-23999
WO 129/4	IY Service No 24000-29799
WO 129/5	IY Service No 29800-35999
WO 129/6	IY Service No 36000-42199
WO 129/7	IY Service No 42200-45124

H W V 80,000 12—99 Form
B. 111.
8-58-47   1

Army Form B. 111.

SHORT SERVICE.
(One year with the Colours.)
ATTESTATION OF

No. *12*   Name *Louis John Sawyer*   Corps *Imperial Yeomanry*

Questions to be put to the Recruit before Enlistment.

1. What is your Name? .... 1. *Louis John Sawyer*
2. In or near what Parish or Town were you born? .... { 2. In the Parish of *Newmarket* in or near the Town of .... in the County of *Gloucester*
3. Are you a British Subject? .... 3. *Yes*
4. What is your Age? .... 4. *23* Years *7* Months.
5. What is your Trade or Calling? .... 5. *Clerk*
6. Have you resided out of your Father's house for three years continuously in the same place, or occupied a house or land of the yearly value of £10 for one year, and paid rates for the same, and, in either case, if so, state where? .... 6. *No*

You are hereby warned that if after enlistment it is found that you have given a wilfully false answer to any of the following seven questions, you will be liable to a punishment of two years' imprisonment with hard labour.

7. Are you, or have you been, an Apprentice? if so, where? to whom? and for what period? .... 7. *Yes*
8. Are you Married? .... 8. *No*
9. Have you ever been sentenced to Imprisonment by the Civil Power? .... 9. *No*
10. Do you now belong to Her Majesty's Army, the Marines, the Militia, the Militia Reserve, the Royal Navy, the Volunteers, the Yeomanry, the Army Reserve, or the Naval Reserve Force? If so, to what Corps? .... 10. *Yes Yeomanry*
*11. Have you ever served in Her Majesty's Army, the Marines, the Militia, the Militia Reserve, or the Royal Navy? If so, state which and cause of discharge .... 11. *No*
12. Have you truly stated the whole, if any, of your previous Service? .... 12. *Yes*
13. Have you ever been rejected as unfit for Her Majesty's Service? If so, on what grounds? .... 13. *No*
14. Are you willing to be vaccinated or re-vaccinated? .... 14. *Yes*
15. For what Corps are you willing to be enlisted, or are you willing to be enlisted for General Service? .... 15. *Imperial Yeomanry*
16. Did you receive a Notice, and do you understand its meaning, and who gave it to you? .... 16. *Yes* { Name .... Corps *R. Wilts Yeo*

17. Are you willing to serve upon the following conditions provided Her Majesty should so long require your services?

(a) For a term of one year, unless the War in South Africa lasts longer than one year, in which case you will be detained until the War is over. If, however, the war is over in less than one year, you may either be discharged at once or remain until you have completed a year's service, at your option .... 17. *Yes*

I, *Louis John Sawyer* do solemnly declare that the above answers made by me to the above questions are true, and that I am willing to fulfil the engagements made.

Louis John Sawyer SIGNATURE OF RECRUIT.

Signature of Witness.

OATH TO BE TAKEN BY RECRUIT ON ATTESTATION.

I, *Louis John Sawyer* do make Oath, that I will be faithful and bear true Allegiance to Her Majesty, Her Heirs, and Successors, and that I will, as in duty bound, honestly and faithfully defend Her Majesty, Her Heirs, and Successors, in Person, Crown, and Dignity against all enemies, and will observe and obey all orders of Her Majesty, Her Heirs, and Successors, and of the Generals and Officers set over me. So help me God.

CERTIFICATE OF MAGISTRATE OR ATTESTING OFFICER.

The Recruit above-named was cautioned by me that if he made any false answer to any of the above questions he would be liable to be punished as provided in the Army Act.
The above questions were then read to the recruit in my presence.
I have taken care that he understands each question, and that his answer to each question has been duly entered as replied to, and the said recruit has made and signed the declaration and taken the oath before me at *Trowbridge* on this *28th* day of *Decr* 1899.

Signature of the Justice *Batt*

If any alteration is required on this page of the Attestation, a Justice of the Peace should be requested to make it and initial the alteration under Section 80 (6), Army Act.
The Recruit should, if he require it, receive a copy of the Declaration on Army Form B. 112.

side note: * If so, the Recruit is to be asked the particulars of his former Service, and to produce, if possible, his Parchment Certificate of Discharge and Certificate of Character, which should be returned to him conspicuously endorsed on the (Date) in red ink, as follows, viz. —(Name) re-enlisted in the (Regiment)

Fig 8. The Imperial Yeomanry attestation form for Trooper L J Sawyer, 1 (Wiltshire) Company Imperial Yeomanry, 1899. (WO 128/1)

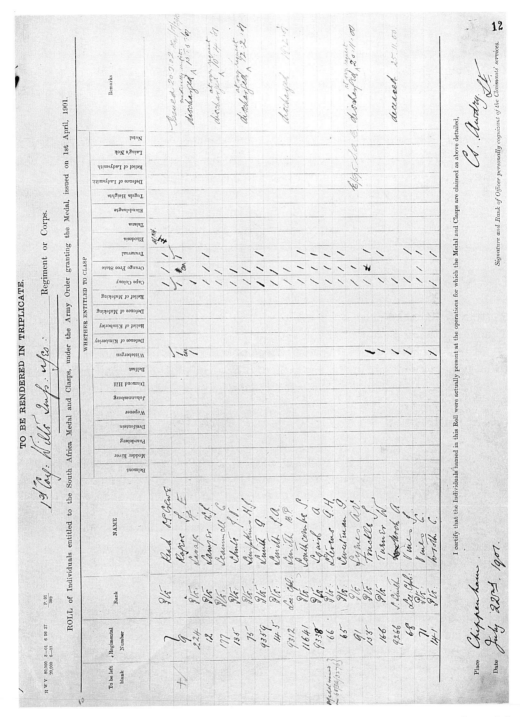

Fig 9. The medal roll showing those members of the 1 (Wiltshire) Company Imperial Yeomanry, entitled to the Queen's South Africa medal for service in the Boer War, 1902. (WO 100/120)

Each register is internally indexed by letter of the surname. If you do not know the service number of the Imperial Yeoman, you will need to consult each index until you find the name and service number of the individual whom you are seeking. If the service number is known, then all that is necessary is for the box of WO 128 which contains the service number of the individual to be ordered on the document ordering computer.

In the case where the individual has a common surname, you may need to look at a number of records of service, checking details of age, place of birth, next of kin and place of enlistment before the correct individual is identified.

Although many men only served in the Imperial Yeomanry, some men transferred to the regular army. The records of those Imperial Yeomen who went on to serve in the regular army and who were discharged before 1914 may be found in the class WO 97.

6.3.2 Officers

Apart from the records mentioned in 6.2 above, details relating to the service of Imperial Yeomanry officers are more difficult to obtain. Although no records of service exist, it is possible to obtain details from the 'war services' section in the January 1901 and 1902 *Army List* and from the nominal roll of officers in WO 129/12. All commissions in the Imperial Yeomanry were announced in the London Gazette (PRO Class ZJ 1).

6.4 Medals

Many officers and men of the Imperial Yeomanry who saw service in South Africa qualified for the Queen's South Africa Medal (QSA) and the King's South Africa Medal (KSA). The medal rolls for the QSA awarded to the Imperial Yeomanry are in WO 100/120-130 (see **Figure 9**) and the medal rolls for the KSA in WO 100/356-357. Both medal rolls are available on microfilm. The Imperial Yeomanry QSA and KSA medal rolls are arranged by battalion. As individuals served in Imperial Yeomanry companies, it is necessary to know which company was in which battalion. Appendix 4 lists all companies who served in South Africa and which battalion they served in.

The Imperial Yeomanry Long Service and Good Conduct Medal was instituted in 1904 as a reward to NCOs and Troopers for ten years exemplary service. Awards of the medal were announced in Army Orders (WO 123). The award was made obsolete in 1908 on the formation of the Territorial Force. Some 1674 medals were awarded.

7. THE TERRITORIAL ARMY

7.1 Introduction

Pursuant to the Territorial and Reserve Forces Act 1907, which came into force on 18 March 1908, the Militia was replaced by the Special Reserve. Conditions of service for officers of the Militia joining the Special Reserve, 1907 and 1908, are set out in papers in WO 32/8597-8599 (under code 59A). In 1910 a committee was formed for the organization of the Special Reserve: it reported that year and the following year (WO 32/8603-8605 (under code 14J)). At the same time, the Yeomanry and Volunteers became the Territorial Force (from 1921, the Territorial Army), administered by County Associations. The overall direction of the new auxiliary forces belonged to the Director General of the Territorial Forces, later to the Director General of the Territorial Army. Development of the Territorials was entrusted to the Territorial Force Advisory Council, for which the following records have survived:

1906-1908*	WO 32/9234-9241	(under code 57A)
1908	WO 32/9696	(under code 6A)
1910	WO 32/9697	(under code 6A)
1914	WO 32/9698	(under code 6A)
1927	WO 32/9699	(under code 6A)
1935-1946	WO 32/9670	(under code 6A)

* Matters concerning provision and planning.

The Council's task included, in addition to establishing matters of general policy for the Territorials and the drawing up of Regulations, such matters as their formation, staffing and manning.

Alongside the regular Territorial Forces, and in accordance with the provisions of s7(6) of the Territorial and Reserve Forces Act 1907, the War Office, between 1908 and 1910, elaborated plans for the creation of a Territorial Force Reserve in three classes: the Territorial Force Reserve, the Technical Reserve and the Veteran Reserve. The *King's Regulations* covering all three branches were issued with Special Army Order, May 1910, presented to both Houses of Parliament, 9 June 1910, and published that same year in London by His Majesty's Stationery Office. The papers are in WO 32/6585. Provisional Orders concerning the Cadet Units were also included.

In 1921 the Special Reserve was re-named the Militia, which in 1924 became the Supplementary Reserve. The Supplementary Reserve Regulations, 1947 to 1951, are in WO 32 (under code 57B).

Post-war conditions of service for volunteers, both as Territorial Army Officer and other ranks, were examined in files stretching from 1945 to 1948 (WO 32/12868 (under code 59A)).

7.2 General Records

Very few records of the Territorial Forces or Territorial Army have been transferred to the Public Record Office. Those that have been so deposited include the following.

The Territorial Army Precedent Books, 1911 to 1957, are in WO 70/23, 26.

Records of property and finance, 1903 to 1951, are in WO 70/27-30, 32. Other TA records concerning property, taxes and the transfer to the Territorials of lands belonging to the Volunteers and Yeomanry are among the registered papers of the War Office in WO 32 (under code 6D). Returns showing Headquarters of Units and Outlying Drill Stations, 1913, are in WO 114/55. Records of Territorial finances are also to be found in WO 32 (under code 6H).

Records concerning the organization of the Territorials are in WO 32 (see under codes 6 and 14K). Weekly strength returns for home forces are among the Strength Returns of the Army: for September 1914 to November 1920 they are in WO 114/33-51, 56; monthly returns for Territorials' service abroad, November 1914 to December 1917, are in WO 114/52-54. Records concerning titles and distinctions of units are in WO 32 (code 15B), honours and designations of units are in WO 32 (code 16F), and regimental colours and badges in WO 32 (code 43H).

Some Orders of Battle for Territorials have been identified among general army records: WO 32/12775 contains the Mobilization Order of Battle, 1948 to 1950 (2nd revision). The records of the 5th and 6th revisions, 1954 to 1963, and other Mobilization Orders of Battle are believed to be in record class WO 33. They are not specifically identified in the class lists. The Orders of Battle for the Territorial Army Supplementary Reserve, 1950 to 1967, are in WO 32/13821-13826 (under code 6A). Records relating to the anti-aircraft and coastal defence responsibilities of the Territorials are in WO 32 (under code 6C).

The history of the Territorial Force during the First World War, and records concerning its organization, training and relation with the Volunteers, 1914 to 1918, are in WO 161/104 to 112. In 1949 C.3 Branch, War Office: Department of the Permanent Under Secretary of State, produced a number of historical monographs for the use of students at Staff Colleges; including, a study on the wartime contribution of the Territorials: Auxiliary Territorial Service, 1939 to 1945 (WO 277/6).

WO 70/31 is a file of miscellanea relating to the Territorials.

The records of the Territorial and Auxiliary Forces Association, 1946 to 1964, are in WO 70/33; Scottish TAFA records are held in the Scottish Record Office in record class MD 7. Other records concerning the membership, tenure of office, regulations, activities and finance of the Territorial Army County Associations are in WO 32 (under code 6D).

Records concerning the regulations, colours and badges of the Officers Training Corps and of the Cadet Corps are in WO 32 (under code 6F). The papers of the Directorate of the Territorial Army and Army Cadet Force, January to May 1946, are in WO 165/105, among the war diaries of War Office Directorates. The status of the Cadets was examined in 1946 and 1947, and the relative papers are in WO 32/11848 (under code 14J). The legal status of the Officers' Training Corps and the Corps' Regulations had been settled in the early years, 1910 and 1911 (WO 32/8675 (under code 14J)). The qualifications and training of officers of the Territorial Army and the Officers' Training Corps had early been a matter of concern, 1907 and 1908, when the draft regulations of the latter were being drawn up and commented upon (WO 32/6566-6569 (under code 59A)).

Among the records of the specialized Territorial units have been preserved those concerning the project for a Territorial Army Medical Corps in 1907 (WO 32 (under code 14F)); the location of medical units of the Territorials in 1908 (WO 32/6558 (under code 6K)); and the redesignation of the Territorial Army Medical Units between 1950 and 1960 (WO 32/13874 (under code 6A)). Those concerning the Royal Monmouthshire Royal Engineers (Militia) are in WO 32/13860 (under code 6A).

Locations of TA Drill Halls between 1936 and 1944 can be found in WO 379/17.

As can be clearly seen, the records discussed in this section are very fragmented. Many are presumed to be still held by the regiment (or successor regiment) that created them.

7.3 Service Records

The regulations governing the appointment, promotion and retirement of officers of the Territorial Force, 1907 and 1908, are in WO 32/6544 (under code 59A). The basis of selection of officers to command Regular and Territorial Army divisions, 1919, is set out in WO 32/5955 (under code 59E).

The service records of Territorial Army personnel who saw service in the First World War are slowly being released into the custody of the Public Record Office. For information relating to these records see chapter 8.

7.4 Medals and Awards

Records concerning the Territorial Decoration (TD) are in WO 32 (under code 50L). Although the award of the Territorial Decoration to an individual was announced in the London Gazette (PRO ZJ 1), no rolls of the TD are in the custody of the Public Record Office.

Rules for the award of the Territorial Efficiency Medal and of the Territorial Decoration, 1900 to 1903, are in WO 32 (under code 6A). Territorial Army records concerning Decorations and Ceremonial are also to be found in WO 32 (under code 6G).

Other ranks who served for twelve years with good conduct were eligible for the award of the Territorial Force Efficiency Medal (TFEM) (1908-1921) and Territorial Efficiency Medal (TEM) (1921-1930). A microfiche card index for the TFEM is available in the Microfilm Reading Room. Service during the First World War counted as double time towards these awards, consequently it was possible to qualify for a TFEM after only eight years service.

Those men of the Special Reserve who completed fifteen years service and attended fifteen training camps were eligible for the Special Reserve Long Service and Good Conduct Medal. The medal roll for this award is in WO 102/23.

In 1930 both the Territorial Decoration (TD) and the Territorial Efficiency Medal (TEM) were replaced by new awards. The Efficiency Decoration (ED) and the Efficiency Medal were available to eligible officers and other ranks respectively. The Efficiency Medal replaced not only the TEM but also the Militia Long Service and Good Conduct Medal and the Special Reserve Long Service and Good Conduct Medal. Apart from announcements of the award of the ED in the London Gazette (PRO class ZJ 1), there are no rolls for the Efficiency Medal.

In the case of the many territorials who saw service during the First World War, if they received any campaign medals and a TFEM or TEM, details of these awards are sometimes annotated on their medal index cards. See chapter 8 for further details relating to the First World War.

For information about army medal entitlements in general, see the PRO Records Information Leaflets 101 *World War One Service Medal Rolls*, 105 *World War One Gallantry Medals Indexes* and 108 *Records of Medals*.

7.5 Operational Records

For operational records of the First World War period see chapter 8. For operational records of the Second World War period see chapter 10.

8. FIRST WORLD WAR SERVICE

8.1 Introduction

At its peak in March 1918, the British Army had in its ranks, over three million men and women in uniform. The majority of those serving were doing so for the duration of the war only. Many of the men who served between 1914 and 1918 were pre-war territorials, former militiamen and special reservists.

8.2 Records of Service

Officers and other ranks of the Militia, Territorial Force and Yeomanry had all originally enlisted for service in the United Kingdom only. The only members of these forces who served overseas during the First World War were those men who consented to do so. Examples of these consent forms (Army Form E 624) can sometimes be found in the records of service. Examples of a 1914 and a 1916 Army Form E 624 showing the changes made to the agreement the TA soldiers signed, agreeing to serve overseas, can be seen in **Figures 10** and **11**.

8.2.1 Other Ranks

Please note that although over three million personnel saw service in the British Army during the First World War, many records were destroyed by enemy action in 1940. All surviving records for those men who did not continue to serve after 1920 will be made available at the PRO by the year 2003.

There are two different War Office record classes which contain records of service for those men who saw service in the First World War.

WO 364 contains the records of service of 750,000 individuals, all of whom survived their service. Many of the records are for those men who were discharged as a result of sickness or wounds contracted or received during the war. Many records within this class are for pre First World War regulars who were recalled for service between 1914 and 1918. This record class is arranged alphabetically by surname and is available on 4915 reels of microfilm in the Microfilm Reading Room.

WO 363, also on microfilm, contains the records of service of two million individuals, many of whom lost their lives during the war but the majority of whom survived. Once again these records are roughly in alphabetical order. Unlike WO 364 which is arranged in alphabetical order and in one numerical sequence, the first piece of the class (WO 364/1) being a surname beginning with 'A' and the last piece, a surname beginning with 'Z' (WO 364/4915), WO 363 is arranged by letter of the alphabet and then each

'C' Coy

Army Form E. 624.

AGREEMENT to be made by an officer or man of the Territorial Force to subject himself to liability to serve in any place outside the United Kingdom in the event of National emergency.

I (No.)_____905_____ (Rank)__*Private*__

(Name)_____*Spencer J*_____ of the

(Unit) **22nd. Btn. Lndn. Regt**_____do hereby agree,

subject to the conditions stated overleaf, to accept liability, in the event of national emergency, to serve in any place outside the United Kingdom, in accordance with the provisions of Section XIII. (2) (a) of the Territorial and Reserve Forces Act, 1907.

_____*J. Spencer*_____
Signature of Officer or Man.

_____*As. Howe Capt.*_____
Signature of Commanding Officer.

Station__**St Albans**_____

Date____SEP 14 1914_____

W.5843 350,000 1—10 N W V Form
E. 624

Fig 10. A 1914 example of an Army Form E 624 signed by all members of the Territorial Army who consented to serve overseas in the unit they enlisted in, in accordance with the Territorial Army Act 1907. (WO 364/3886)

Army Form E. 624.

IMPERIAL AND GENERAL SERVICE OBLIGATION.

Agreement to be made by an officer or man of the Territorial Force to subject himself to liability to serve in any place outside the United Kingdom during the present period of embodiment.

I (No.) *127* (Rank) *Company Sergt. Major.*

(Name) *William Spencer.* do hereby agree to accept liability, during the present period of embodiment, to serve in any place outside the United Kingdom, in accordance with the provisions of Section XIII. (2) (a) of the Territorial and Reserve Forces Act, 1907, [and where, with a view to service overseas, my transfer to another corps is required, I hereby consent to such transfer notwithstanding that the corps to which I am to be transferred may be different from that in which I am serving].* I understand that release from this obligation can during the present period of embodiment be granted only with the consent of the competent military authority.

This undertaking is given on the understanding that I shall not by reason of such transfer suffer any reduction of the pay and allowances of which I was in receipt immediately prior to transfer.

William Pritchard Spencer (Signature of officer or man.)

(Signature of Commanding Officer.)

(Station) *Crowborough*

(Date) *29th May 1916*

* In the case of an officer the words in brackets should be omitted.

Fig 11. A 1916 example of an Army Form E 624 signed by those members of the Territorial Army who enlisted after 1915, and who agreed to serve overseas and in whatever unit necessary should the Army wish to change their unit.

letter is numbered from 1 onwards. The document reference for an individual piece within WO 363 will look like this, WO 363/A1 or WO 363/F125.

At the time of writing (July 1997) the first reel of WO 363 had not yet been made available in the Microfilm Reading Room but it is anticipated that surnames beginning with the letter 'Z' will be the first to be released and these will have references WO 363/ Z1 - WO 363/Z5.

Records of service for those women who served in the Territorial Force Nursing Service are still in the hands of the Ministry of Defence (see Appendix 6, F.1).

The record class PIN 26 is a collection of disability pension files relating to servicemen who were medically discharged as a result of sickness or wounds. The class contains just over 20,000 files and should be ordered via the document ordering computer. It is arranged in alphabetical order and separated into other ranks, officers and nurses.

8.2.2 Officers

Records of officers who saw service during the First World War will be released in January 1998. If an officer saw service after 1920 his records may not be available as part of this release.

The records of officers are also in two record classes. WO 374 is in alphabetical order by surname and contains just over 77,000 files; and WO 339, is arranged by personal identification number (not a service number but an administrative number), and contains over 120,000 files. WO 338 is an alphabetical index which provides the personal number for use with WO 339. WO 338 will be available on microfilm in the Microfilm Reading Room. The files in WO 339 and WO 374 will be available in their original form and will need to be ordered via document ordering computers. Both of the two record classes contain the files of pre-war regulars, territorials and duration of the war only officers. The records of those officers who were killed in action or who died in service are also in these classes.

Three volumes containing details of officers who served in the 3 Battalion Wiltshire Regiment (Special Reserve) between 1914 and 1918 can be found in WO 76/532-533.

8.3 Medals

Those individuals, including women, who served in an operational theatre during the First World War should have received at least two campaign medals. The medal rolls for campaign medals granted for service between 1914 and 1919 are in the record class WO 329, with an alphabetical index on microfiche in the record class WO 372. It is possible by consulting the index and the medal rolls to ascertain what medals individuals qualified for, which operational theatre they first served in and when they first went overseas.

Further details relating to medals and awards granted for gallantry and for campaign service during the First World War and how the records are used can be found in S Fowler, W Spencer and S Tamblin, *Army Records of the First World War*, PRO Publications, 1996. However, one of the campaign medals granted during the First World War was awarded to members of the Territorial Force only and deserves further explanation.

The Territorial Force War Medal 1914-1919 was awarded to men and women who were members of the Territorial Force on or prior to 30 September 1914 and who served in an operational theatre between 5 August 1914 and 11 November 1918. Those individuals who received either the 1914 Star or 1914/15 Star were not eligible for this award.

8.4 Operations

Although there are many different records which contain details relating to operations, the most useful are probably the Unit War Diaries in WO 95 and WO 154. The Unit War Diary provides, on a day to day basis, details about the activities of an individual unit, whether they are in action, under training (in an operational theatre) or at rest. Few individuals are mentioned by name, and these are usually officers.

It is useful when using WO 95 to know the date on which an individual unit entered an operational theatre. Details relating to when a regiment went overseas, which theatres they served in and which division or brigade they served in can be found in E A James, *British Infantry Regiments, 1914-1918*, (Naval and Military Press, London 1993) a copy of which is available in the Microfilm Reading Room.

Other operational records include: Trench Maps in WO 153, WO 297, WO 298 and WO 302; Headquarters papers in WO 158; and Intelligence Summaries in WO 157.

8.5 Casualties

Although it is possible to find details relating to the operations in which individuals died by consulting the Unit War Diary, unless the dead individual is an officer, very few are mentioned by name.

Soldiers Died in The Great War and *Officers Died in The Great War* are two publications produced by HMSO after the First World War. These works list casualties by regiment and battalion and then in alphabetical order, each work giving date of death but only place of death being provided for other ranks. *Soldiers Died* is available on microfilm and both works are available in the Microfilm Reading Room.

It is possible to obtain the details of where an individual is buried or commemorated from the Commonwealth War Graves Commission. See Appendix 6 for the address.

Further details relating to all of the records discussed in this chapter can be found in S Fowler, W Spencer and S Tamblin, *Army Service Records of the First World War*, (PRO Publications, 1996). A copy of this can be found in the Microfilm Reading Room and Research Enquiries Room.

9. THE HOME GUARD

In 1940 the Home Guard (originally the Local Defence Volunteers) was formed for home defence; it was dissolved in 1945. The officers' terms of service in the Home Defence battalions were set out in 1941 in WO 32/9979 (under code 59A). Personal records and enrolment forms (Army Form W 3066), which are closed for 75 years, are in the custody of the Army Medal Office at Droitwich, and information from them is only provided to next of kin or to individuals interested in their own service in the Home Guard (for address see Appendix 6, F.2). Other Home Guard papers may survive in county record offices among the Territorial Army County Associations' records or in private collections, and others may have been deposited with service records in the Army Medal Office.

Once the Home Guard was established, *Home Guard Lists* similar in format to the conventional *Army Lists* were produced. *Home Guard Lists* from September 1941 - October 1944 are kept together with a set of the Army Lists in the PRO library. Dates of commission and appointments are given, and indications of regimental and Territorial Army postings. In October 1944 several volumes were issued containing the final list of Home Guard officers (WO 199/310-3217, see **Figure 12**). These lists are identical to the October 1944 *Home Guard List.*

The Southern Region Home Guard, 1941 to 1945, received considerable attention in railway records: see the publications collected together in British Transport Historical Records, Periodical, Newspapers and Magazines, in record class ZPER 96.

Among the Military Headquarters' Papers, 1939 to 1945 (WO 199), are histories and miscellaneous papers of some Home Guard units. See Appendix 5 for a full list of Home Guard unit histories.

Civil Defence came under the jurisdiction of the Ministry of Home Security. In the Registered Files concerning Air Raid Precautions (ARP GEN) created by Home Security (HO 186 and the parallel records in HO 207) are records concerning the Home Guard and other Civil Defence organizations (for both males and females). There is a subject index at the beginning of the record class lists. Another series of records relating to the Home Guard is in HO 199, the Intelligence Branch Registered Files, 1939 to 1950.

Under code 66 of WO 32 will be found the general series of registered papers concerning the Home Guard: they are case papers of a generally historical nature, records of legislation, uniforms, pay and allowances. WO 33/1700 concerns Home Guard equipment, 1942 to 1944. Finally, there is a committee report, dated October 1940, in WO 163/414, among the War Office Council and Army Council records. Other related sets of papers are in the Historical Section Files (Archivist and Librarian Series) of the Cabinet Office, which are in record class CAB 106, together with the Ministry of Defence

```
                    ANTI-AIRCRAFT COMMAND - contd.           7

                    NO.1 H.G. A.A. REGIMENT - contd.
```

71 HAMPSHIRE AND ISLE OF WIGHT H.G.
        H.A.A. BATTERY

Major
Pannell, J. P. M., M.B.E.   4/ 1/43

Captains		2nd Lieutenants	
Jackson, W. H.	26/ 1/43	Mitchell, T. W. J.	27/ 5/43
West, F. E.	1/ 2/43	Green, A. A.	27/ 5/43
Legat, T. W.	1/ 2/43	Butchers, J. W.	27/ 5/43
Waltho, A. J.	22/12/43	Skuse, H. G.	27/ 5/43
	1/12/42	Lascelles, C. K. B.	27/ 5/43
Evans, C. V.	21/ 4/44	Wiltshire, D. R.	27/ 5/43
		Dawes, B. J.	24/ 6/43
		Howell, F. H.	24/ 6/43
		Martell, R. H. C.	24/ 6/43
Lieutenants		Royal, A. E.	24/ 6/43
King, F. W.	1/ 5/43	Young, A. V.	15/10/43
Hole, L. W.	24/ 6/43	Hoare, H. R.	22/12/43
Sunderland, J. E.	16/ 5/43		10/ 9/43
Lisby, V. C.	22/12/43	Lockwood, F. H.	22/12/43
Timbrell, G. W.	22/12/43		10/12/43
Dunford, H. A.	17/ 2/44	Bell-Simmonds, M. B.	22/12/43
White, A. L.	7/ 4/44		10/ 9/43
Swanson, J. R.	8/ 4/44	Osborne, J. L.	22/12/43
Beynon, I. R.	19/ 4/44		29/ 7/43
Legg, H. S.	19/ 4/44	Rushton, J. W.	22/12/43
Davis, J. S.	22/ 4/44		29/ 7/43
Harrison, F. N.	3/ 5/44	Apsey, H. J. J.	7/ 4/44
	5/ 4/44	Parsons, M. C.	7/ 4/44
Pearcey, W. C.	9/ 5/44	Collins, B. F.	19/ 5/44
Walton, N. A. C.	13/ 5/44	White, H. L.	9/ 6/44
Dunnings, J.	27/ 5/44	Ward, J. W.	9/ 6/44
Pacey, M. G.	27/ 5/44	Hayward, C. N. H.	9/ 6/44
Luker, H. C.	28/ 5/44	Osgood, W. N.	16/ 6/44
Neish, S. A.	30/ 5/44	Reade, J. B.	6/10/44
Newman, A. J. H.	31/ 5/44		
Child, K.	2/ 6/44		
Sheriton, S. E.	10/ 6/44		
Smith, E. F.	26/ 7/44		
Reeves, C. B.	26/ 7/44		
House, W. C. J.	26/ 7/44		
Smart, S. W.	27/ 7/44		
Bishop, L. N.	15/ 8/44		
Dunning, C. W.	15/ 8/44		
Secker, L. H.	15/ 8/44		
Bell-Simmonds, W. H.	18/ 8/44		
Pooley, A. F.	20/ 8/44		

53826-1(11)

Fig 12. Home Guard, Anti-aircraft Command, Final list of Officers, October 1944, 71st Hampshire and Isle of Wight Battery. (WO 199/3210, p 7)

(128A) Sergeant
        Frederick Charles Bennett,
          2nd Som (Taunton) Battalion Home Guard.

        This N.C.O. has worked extremely hard to make himself a
first class instructor in all signals training. He has taken the great-
est interest in all Battalion and Garrison exercises and worked very
hard to make them a success. The efficiency of the Battalion Signals
is in great measure due to the zeal of this N.C.O. He has been a
member of the Home Guard from the days of the L.D.V.

(128B) Corporal
        Francis Herbert Tucker,
          14th Battalion Devon Home Guard.

        This N.C.O. enrolled in the L.D.V. He is lame. By trade he
is a shoeing smith serving a large area. During the whole of his service
he has been indefatigable in carrying out unostentatiously all the
"donkey work" of his platoon, including a lot of administrative work.
In spite of his disability, he has never missed a parade or exercise.
He has set a fine example to his platoon and has been an inspiration
to all.

(128C) Sergeant
        Frederick Dunn,
          8th Cornwall (Helston) Battalion Home Guard.

        Sergeant Dunn is a first class instructor who has taken great
pains to become proficient. He has always been prepared to devote
every spare minute in the cause of Home Guard efficiency. He has, by
his outstanding keenness and good example, done more than any O.R. to
raise the standard of efficiency in this Battalion. He has served
with the Home Guard since 30 May 40.

(129) Sergeant
        William Frederick James, Timbrell,
          5th Som (Bath City) Battalion Home Guard.

        Was an original member of the L.D.V. He is far from strong -
the result of a last was disability - and would never have been able to
carry out strenuous duties as an ordinary member of the Battalion.
Realising this he made the suggestion that he should take over the

Fig 13. A precis of a recommendation taken from an Army Form W 3121, for the award of a British Empire Medal to a member of the Home Guard on stand down in 1944. (AIR 2/9040)

Secretariat Files in CAB 120.

The Operational Papers of the Home Guard are to be found among the records of the Prime Minister's Office, in record class PREM 3[1]. They can be used for identifying the whereabouts of Home Guard units. Home Guard War Diaries are in record class WO 166, War Diaries, Home Forces, 1939 to 1945. Among the war diaries of the War Office Directorates are the reports of the Inspectorate of the Home Guard, June to November 1940, in WO 165/92, followed by the reports of the Directorate of the Home Guard, November 1940 to December 1945, in WO 165/93.

The records concerning the stand-down of the Home Guard in England and similar colonial forces, 1944-1948, are in WO 32/10818 (under code O [A]).

A file containing recommendations for the award of the British Empire Medal to members of the Home Guard on stand-down can be found in AIR 2/ 9040. An example of a recommendation can be seen in **Figure 13**.

Records of local proceedings, usually press cuttings and some private papers, have sometimes been preserved in local record offices.

---

[1] See also the study by LB Whittaker, *Stand Down! Orders of Battle for the units of the Home Guard of the United Kingdom, November 1944* (Newport, 1990).

10. SECOND WORLD WAR SERVICE

10.1 General Records

There are many records relating to the politics and the planning and execution of operations during the Second World War. J Cantwell, *The Second World War: A Guide to Records in the Public Record Office*, HMSO, 1993, contains general descriptions of records relating to this period.

10.2 Operations

Of prime interest to those seeking information about the activities of individual soldiers who saw service between 1939 and 1945 are the Unit War Diaries. Unlike the First World War Unit War Diaries, which are collected in two record classes and then divided into operational theatres, the Unit War Diaries for the Second World War are in separate record classes for each specific operational theatre.

Due to the mobile nature of warfare between 1939 and 1945, it was possible for a unit to serve in a number of different operational theatres. To find out where in the world a unit served, it is necessary to consult H F Joslen, *Orders of Battle of the Second World War*, HMSO, 1960, a copy of which is available in the Research Enquiries Room. Once the operational theatre has been ascertained, the next step is to consult the Unit War Diary record class relevant to that theatre.

After the First World War some territorial units changed from being infantry into artillery and even cavalry. It must be remembered that many yeomanry units changed from horses to tanks and that the Unit War Diaries may be listed under Royal Armoured Corps.

For further information about operational records see PRO Records Information Leaflet 7, *Operational Records of The British Army During the Second World War*.

10.3 Records of Service

Records of service for those men who saw service in the Second World War are still maintained by the Ministry of Defence (see Appendix 6, F.1)

It is possible to obtain a certain amount of information about officers from the *Army List*.

10.4 Casualties

The Roll of Honour listing Army casualties of the Second World War is in WO 304.

Details of where an individual is buried or commemorated can be obtained from the Commonwealth War Graves Commission. See Appendix 6 for the address.

10.5 Medals

10.5.1 Campaign Medals

The Public Record Office holds no medal rolls for campaign medals granted for service in the Second World War. Medal records for operations after 1920 are held by the Ministry of Defence (see Appendix 6, F.2).

10.5.2 Gallantry Awards and Awards Granted for Meritorious Service

Surviving recommendations for awards granted for gallantry or meritorious service are in the record class WO 373. This class, which is available on microfilm, is arranged into a number of different sections: Gallantry, Non-Combat Gallantry and Meritorious Service being the main section headings. Each section is divided into operational theatre and then by gazette date (the date on which the award was announced in the London Gazette).

When using WO 373, it is important to know the type of award eg Military Cross (MC) or Officer of the Order of the British Empire (OBE), the individual was granted; which operational theatre the award was won in and when it was announced in the London Gazette. If this information is not available, it is possible to consult the index for the London Gazette which is available in the Microfilm Reading Room and then order the London Gazette issue (PRO class ZJ 1) in which the award was announced before using WO 373. Once type of award, operational theatre and gazette date are known, WO 373 can be consulted.

Awards granted in Half Yearly Honours Lists (the New Year and Birthday Honours Lists) are also available in WO 373.

Most of the recommendations in WO 373 provide details about the action for which the award was granted. Very few recommendations for Mentioned in Despatches survive; those that do are also in WO 373.

11. CASE STUDIES

11.1 Introduction

The problem with providing case studies illustrating how to use the records is one of continuity, as what has survived can be patchy and types of records change. In order to illustrate the records over a wide chronological range, three Militia case studies covering the late eighteenth to early twentieth centuries and one Imperial Yeomanry case study have been provided.

11.2 John Petty, Warwickshire Militia, 1790-1831

Unlike the regular army, where men serving in a particular regiment could come from many different geographical locations, the majority of the men serving in a Militia regiment came from a much smaller catchment area, usually from within the county under whose name the unit served. When looking for a militiaman from the late eighteenth or early nineteenth centuries, the logical starting point for any search will be the Militia Musters and Pay Lists in WO 13. By consulting the musters for a given period, it is possible to build up a detailed record of service showing, if the musters survive, when an individual joined, where he served, when he was promoted and when he was discharged.

If it was likely that an individual served for over fifteen years, then he was likely to receive a pension. Pension records, in the form of discharge papers, for local militiamen discharged between 1760 and 1854, are in the record class WO 97. A computerized database for these records is available in the Microfilm Reading Room. Consultation of this database led to the discovery of the discharge document for Sergeant John Petty, Warwickshire Militia (WO 97/1106) (illustrated in **Figure 5**). Although the record of service details his service, it does not provide exact dates of promotion, nor details of where he served. The muster and pay lists for the Warwickshire Militia for the whole period that John Petty served do not survive. However, the muster for 1831 (WO 13/2212) actually records his discharge and the payment of 'Marching Money', so that John Petty could go to Chelsea Hospital for his discharge board and be awarded his pension.

Key Points to Note

Use WO 13 (Militia Muster and Pay Lists 1780-1878) to build up a record of service if no record of service exists.

Use the WO 97 database and the records in WO 97/1091-1112 if you think that the individual was discharged to pension before 1855.

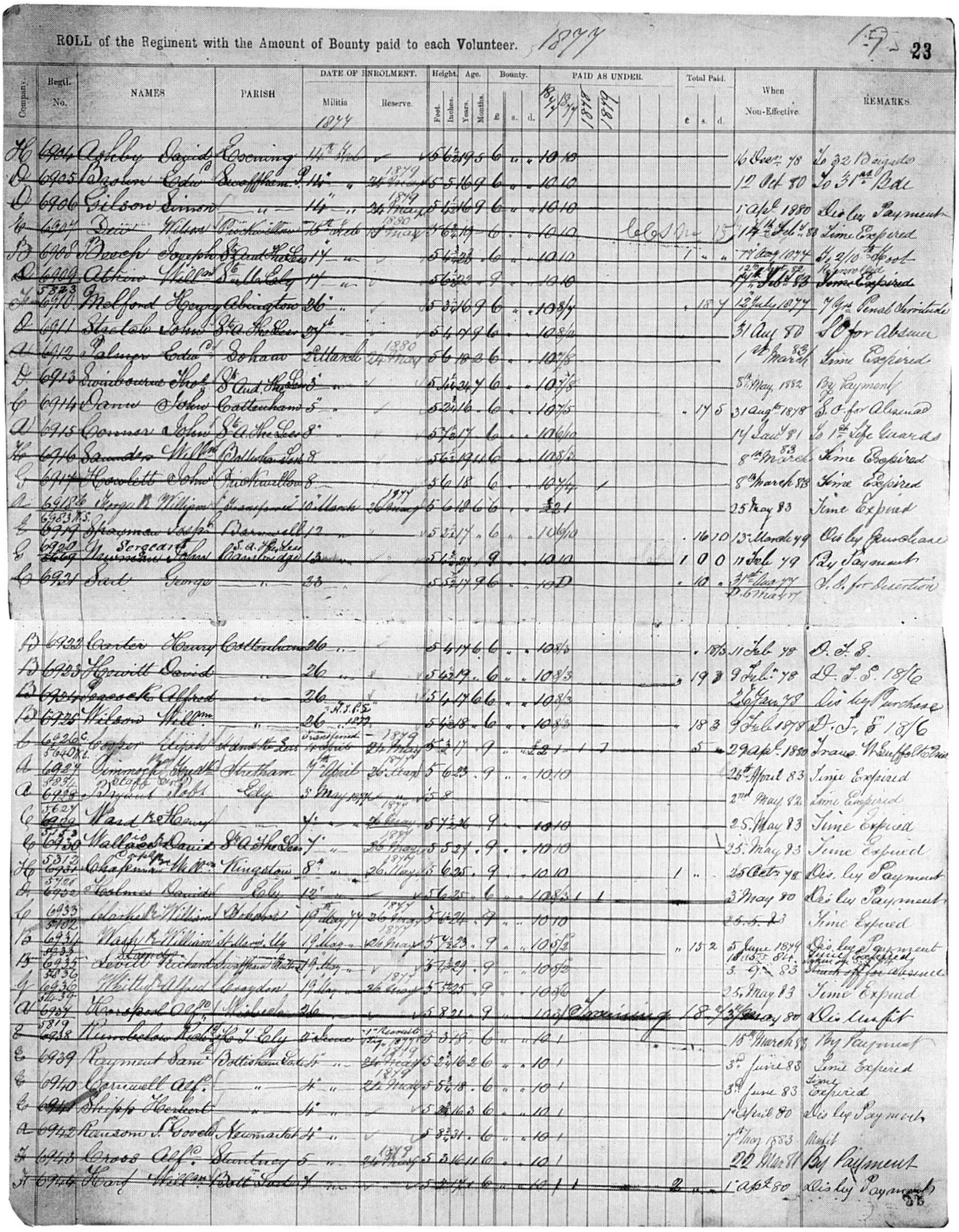

Fig 14. The Bounty Book of the Cambridge Militia, showing the bounties paid to recruits on enlistment between 1875 and 1901. (WO 68/149)

11.3 Robert Bryant (Alias Robert Whitby), Cambridge Militia, 1867-1882

When researching militiamen in the mid to late nineteenth century, it is possible that the individual you are seeking is a member of the Permanent Staff, rather than a volunteer soldier. In cases where an ex regular joins the Permanent Staff, his discharge documents will be filed in WO 97, under the date when he left the regular army and not the Militia.

Robert Bryant (alias Robert Whitby) left the 73 Foot in 1867 and joined the Cambridge Militia as a Permanent Staff Instructor. The discharge papers for this man are in WO 97/1606, which is in the chronological range 1855-1872. Although there are papers relating to his service in the Militia between 1867 and 1882 in his discharge documents, it may be possible to find Robert Bryant on the 1881 census, stating that he was a militiaman. In cases where the date of entry into a Militia unit is unknown, it is possible to discover when an individual joined and left a unit, if the unit Enrolment Books and Bounty Books survive. As these records are specific Militia unit records, should they survive, then they will be in the record class WO 68. The Bounty Books for the Cambridge Militia are in WO 68/148-149 (see **Figure 14**) and they duly record the enrolment of Robert Bryant as Permanent Staff Instructor in 1867 and his final discharge in 1882.

Key Points to Note

Permanent Staff Instructors were usually ex regulars and their records of service are in WO 97, by date of discharge from the regulars, not the Militia.

Use the Militia Records in WO 68 to find out when an individual joined and left a unit.

11.4 Arthur Crabb, 4 Battalion Suffolk Regiment (Cambridge Militia) 1899-1907

Attestation records for the Militia are in the record class WO 96. Although the date range of the attestation records varies according to regiment, the majority are late nineteenth or early twentieth century.

The records in WO 96 are arranged by Militia Unit and then alphabetically by surname.

The attestation papers for Arthur Crabb are in WO 96/246 (see **Figure 15**) and, much as the records in WO 97 do, they provide date of joining, physical description, if and when the individual was promoted, if he received any medals and when he was discharged.

It is possible in some cases to find out where an individual actually served by consulting the Muster and Pay Lists in WO 13, but because they end in 1878 details of service after that date have to be sought elsewhere.

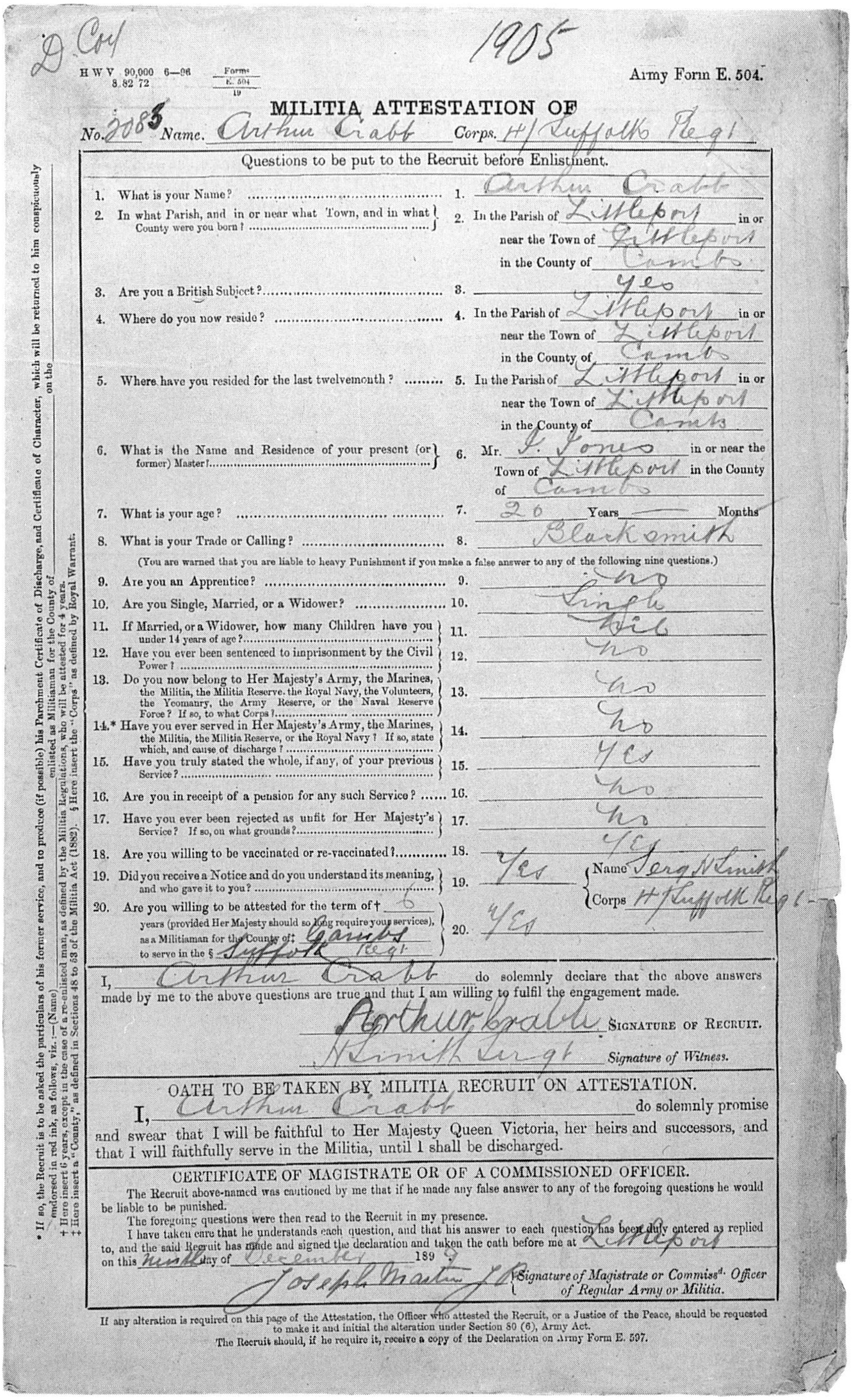

D Coy 1905

H W V 90,000 6—96 8.82 72 Forms E. 504 19

Army Form E. 504.

MILITIA ATTESTATION OF

No. 2085 Name. Arthur Crabb Corps. 4/ Suffolk Regt

Questions to be put to the Recruit before Enlistment.

1. What is your Name? .... 1. Arthur Crabb
2. In what Parish, and in or near what Town, and in what County were you born? .... 2. In the Parish of Littleport in or near the Town of Littleport in the County of Cambs
3. Are you a British Subject? .... 3. Yes
4. Where do you now reside? .... 4. In the Parish of Littleport in or near the Town of Littleport in the County of Cambs
5. Where have you resided for the last twelvemonth? .... 5. In the Parish of Littleport in or near the Town of Littleport in the County of Cambs
6. What is the Name and Residence of your present (or former) Master? .... 6. Mr. J. Jones in or near the Town of Littleport in the County of Cambs
7. What is your age? .... 7. 20 Years — Months
8. What is your Trade or Calling? .... 8. Blacksmith

(You are warned that you are liable to heavy Punishment if you make a false answer to any of the following nine questions.)

9. Are you an Apprentice? .... 9. No
10. Are you Single, Married, or a Widower? .... 10. Single
11. If Married, or a Widower, how many Children have you under 14 years of age? .... 11. Nil
12. Have you ever been sentenced to imprisonment by the Civil Power? .... 12. No
13. Do you now belong to Her Majesty's Army, the Marines, the Militia, the Militia Reserve, the Royal Navy, the Volunteers, the Yeomanry, the Army Reserve, or the Naval Reserve Force? If so, to what Corps? .... 13. No
14.* Have you ever served in Her Majesty's Army, the Marines, the Militia, the Militia Reserve, or the Royal Navy? If so, state which, and cause of discharge? .... 14. No
15. Have you truly stated the whole, if any, of your previous Service? .... 15. Yes
16. Are you in receipt of a pension for any such Service? .... 16. No
17. Have you ever been rejected as unfit for Her Majesty's Service? If so, on what grounds? .... 17. No
18. Are you willing to be vaccinated or re-vaccinated? .... 18. Yes
19. Did you receive a Notice and do you understand its meaning, and who gave it to you? .... 19. Yes Name Sergt H Smith Corps 4/ Suffolk Regt
20. Are you willing to be attested for the term of† 6 years (provided Her Majesty should so long require your services), as a Militiaman for the‡ County of Cambs to serve in the § Suffolk Regt .... 20. Yes

I, Arthur Crabb do solemnly declare that the above answers made by me to the above questions are true, and that I am willing to fulfil the engagement made.

Arthur Crabb SIGNATURE OF RECRUIT.

H Smith Sergt *Signature of Witness.*

OATH TO BE TAKEN BY MILITIA RECRUIT ON ATTESTATION.

I, Arthur Crabb do solemnly promise and swear that I will be faithful to Her Majesty Queen Victoria, her heirs and successors, and that I will faithfully serve in the Militia, until I shall be discharged.

CERTIFICATE OF MAGISTRATE OR OF A COMMISSIONED OFFICER.

The Recruit above-named was cautioned by me that if he made any false answer to any of the foregoing questions he would be liable to be punished.

The foregoing questions were then read to the Recruit in my presence.

I have taken care that he understands each question, and that his answer to each question has been duly entered as replied to, and the said Recruit has made and signed the declaration and taken the oath before me at Littleport on this ninth day of December 1899

Joseph Martin J.P. *Signature of Magistrate or Commissd. Officer of Regular Army or Militia.*

If any alteration is required on this page of the Attestation, the Officer who attested the Recruit, or a Justice of the Peace, should be requested to make it and initial the alteration under Section 80 (6), Army Act.

The Recruit should, if he require it, receive a copy of the Declaration on Army Form E. 597.

* If so, the Recruit is to be asked the particulars of his former service, and to produce (if possible) his Parchment Certificate of Discharge, and Certificate of Character, which will be returned to him conspicuously endorsed in red ink, as follows, viz.:—(Name) .... enlisted as Militiaman for the County of .... on the ....

† Here insert 6 years, except in the case of a re-enlisted man, as defined by the Militia Regulations, who will be attested for 4 years.

‡ Here insert a "County," as defined in Sections 48 to 53 of the Militia Act (1882). § Here insert the "Corps" as defined by Royal Warrant.

Fig 15. The Army Form A 504, Militia Attestation form completed for Arthur Crabb on enlistment into the 4 Battalion Suffolk Regiment (Cambridge Militia) in 1899. (WO 96/246)

The 4 Battalion Suffolk Regiment (Cambridge Militia) records in WO 68 are useful for discovering further information about Arthur Crabb. The Enrolment Book in WO 68/155 confirms his dates of service and also tells us that he served in C Company. The Bounty Book (WO 68/149), although it mentions his name, only confirms information we already have.

Key Points to Note

Although records of service are available in WO 96, further details can be obtained from the Militia Records in WO 68 if an attestation does not survive. If a militiaman joined the Regular Army his record may be in WO 97.

11.5 Louis John Sawyer, 1 Company (Wiltshire) Imperial Yeomanry, 1899-1901

Records of service for men who served in the Imperial Yeomanry are quite easy to locate. The indexes to the papers in WO 128 are in the record class WO 129. See chapter 6 for further details.

The records in WO 128 are similar to the records in WO 96 and WO 97, and they provide similar types of information: place of birth, place of attestation, physical description, details of service, medals awarded and date and place of discharge (see **Figure 8**).

Louis John Sawyer joined the Imperial Yeomanry at Trowbridge in Wiltshire on 28 December 1899. He served in South Africa between 1 March, 1900 and 8 July, 1901, qualifying for the Queen's South Africa Medal with 4 clasps (see **Figure 9**). Louis Sawyer was discharged on 15 July 1901.

Key Points to Note

Records of service for the Imperial Yeomanry are in WO 128, with indexes in WO 129.

It is possible to obtain some details from the Queen's South Africa Medal rolls in WO 100, including in some cases dates of discharge.

In some cases, men of the Imperial Yeomanry transferred into the Regular Army. The indexes of service numbers (WO 129) record if a man transferred into the Regular Army, as in some cases do the medal rolls for the Queen's South Africa Medal.

12. BIBLIOGRAPHY

Many units have been the object of an historical study. Users should seek guidance thereto in a major research library. Some general works are listed below.

I F W Becket, *Riflemen Form! A Study of the Rifle Volunteer Movement, 1859-1908*. Aldershot: The Ogilby Trust, 1982.

S Fowler, W Spencer and S Tamblin, *Army Service Records of the First World War*, PRO Publications, 1996.

J Gibson and M Medlycott, *Militia Lists and Musters, 1757-1876*, 2nd edn, Birmingham: Federation of Family History Societies, 1990.

W G Hoskins, *Exeter Militia Lists, 1803*, London and Chichester: Phillimore on behalf of Devon and Cornwall Record Society, 1972.

E A James, *British Infantry Regiments, 1914-1918*, Liverpool Medal Company, 1995.

H F Joslen, *Orders of Battle of the Second World War*, 1939-1945, HMSO, 1960.

H McAnally, *The Irish Militia, 1793-1818*, Dublin: Clonmore: Reynolds, and London: Eyre and Spotiswood, 1949.

B Owen, *Welsh Militia and Volunteer Corps, 1757-1908*, Caernarfon: Palace Books. Under that general title has been published to date: vol 1: *Anglesey and Caernarfonshire*, 1989, and vol 2: *The Glamorgan Regiments of Militia*, 1990.

H J Owen, *Merioneth Volunteers and Local Militia during the Napoleonic Wars (1795-1816)*, Dolgelley: Hughes Brothers [1934].

G A Steppler, *Britons, To arms! The story of the British Volunteer Soldier and the Volunteer Tradition in Leicestershire and Rutland*, Worcester: Sutton, 1992.

R Westlake, *The Volunteer Infantry, 1880-1908*, London: Military Historical Society, 1992.

R Westlake and M Chappell, *British Territorial Units, 1914-18* (Men-at-Arms Series, n° 245), London: Osprey, 1991.

R J Weston, *The English Militia in the Eighteenth Century. The Story of a Political Issue, 1660-1802*, London: Routledge and Kegan Paul, and Toronto: University of Toronto Press, 1960.

APPENDIX 1

ORGANIZATIONAL STRUCTURE OF THE MILITIA FROM 1759

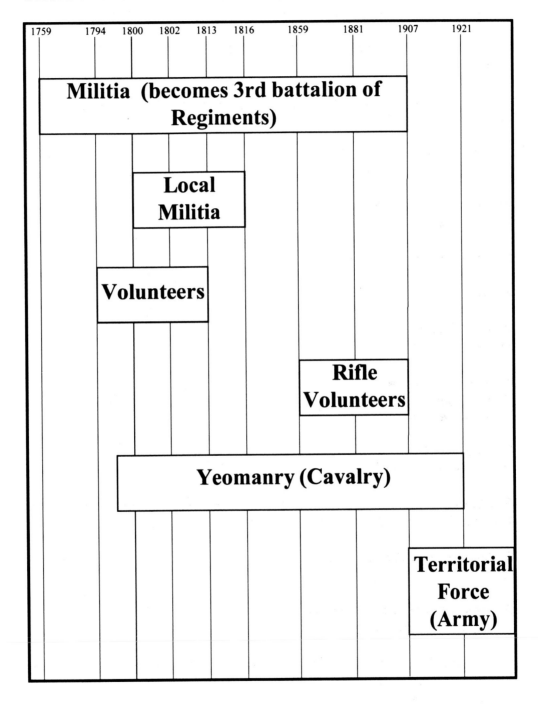

APPENDIX 2

NAMES OF DISTRICTS OF MILITIA IN ENGLAND AND WALES

Anglesey
Bedfordshire
Berkshire
Brecon
Buckinghamshire
Cambridgeshire
Cardiganshire
Carmarthenshire
Caernarfonshire
Cheshire
Cornwall
Cumberland
Denbighshire
Derbyshire
Devon, East
Devon, North
Devon, South
Dorsetshire
Durham
Essex, East
Essex, West
Flintshire
Glamorganshire
Gloucester, North
Gloucester, South
Hants, North
Hants, South
Hants, Isle of Wight
Herefordshire
Hertfordshire
Huntingdonshire
Kent, East
Kent, West
Lancashire, First
Lancashire, Second
Lancashire, Third
Leicestershire
Lincoln, North

Lincoln, South
London
Merionethshire
Middlesex, East
Middlesex, West
Middlesex, Westminster
Monmouth
Montgomeryshire
Norfolk, East
Norfolk, West
Northamptonshire
Northumberland
Nottinghamshire
Oxfordshire
Pembrokeshire
Radnorshire
Rutlandshire
Shropshire
Somerset, First
Somerset, Second
Staffordshire
Suffolk, East
Suffolk, West
Surrey, First
Surrey, Second
Sussex
Tower Hamlets, First
Tower Hamlets, Second
Warwickshire
Westmorland
Wiltshire
Worcestershire
York, East Riding
York, North Riding
York, West Riding, First
York, West Riding, Second
York, West Riding, Third

APPENDIX 3

NAMES OF MILITIA UNITS BEFORE AND AFTER THE CARDWELL REFORMS WITH REFERENCES TO SURVIVING REGIMENTAL BOOKS

One of the effects of the Cardwell Reforms of the regular army was to bring it into line with the county based Militia. It was thence a short distance to amalgamating the two, but not in such a way that their identities were lost. Each County Regiment of the regular army, in theory at least, comprised a battalion for posting anywhere in the Empire, while a second battalion became the depot battalion, which remained at home. The Militia now became a third, and if need be, a fourth, battalion of the County Regiment, and for the most part changed its name.

NAME OF REGIMENT	REFERENCE
Aberdeenshire Militia, Royal *became* 3rd Bn Gordon Highlanders	WO 76/451-452
Amounderness Battalion, Lancashire Militia	WO 79/2
Anglesey Militia, Royal	WO 25/3920
Argyll and Bute Artillery Militia *became* West of Scotland Royal Field (Reserve) Artillery	WO 68/98-117
Argyll and Sutherland Highlanders, 4th Bn *formerly* Royal Renfrew Militia	WO 68/372-374
Armagh Militia *became* 3rd Bn Royal Irish Fusiliers	WO 68/383-401
Armagh Light Infantry *became* 3rd Bn Royal Irish Fusiliers	WO 68/476
Army Service Corps	WO 68/562
Bedfordshire Regiment, 4th Bn *formerly* Hertfordshire Militia	WO 68/375
Berkshire Militia *became* 3rd Bn Berkshire Regiment	WO 68/472

Berwick Artillery Militia *became* part of South East of Scotland Royal Field (Reserve) Artillery	WO 68/78-85
Border Regiment, 3rd Bn *formerly* Royal Cumberland Militia	WO 68/376
Border Regiment, 4th Bn *formerly* Royal Westmorland Militia	WO 68/377
Buckinghamshire Militia, Royal *became* 3rd Bn Oxfordshire Light Infantry	WO 68/242-256
Bute, Argyll and Artillery Militia *became* West of Scotland Royal Field (Reserve) Artillery	WO 68/98-117
Caernarvon and Merioneth Militia, Royal *became* 4th Bn Royal Welch Fusiliers	WO 68/215-217
Cambridge Militia *became* 4th Bn Suffolk Regiment	WO 68/140-157
Cameron Highlanders, 3rd Bn *formerly* Inverness and Highland Light Infantry Militia	WO 68/378
Cardigan Royal Field (Reserve) Artillery *formerly* Cardigan Royal Rifles Militia	WO 68/1-2
Carlow Militia *became* 8th Bn King's Royal Rifle Corps	WO 68/296-305 WO 76/289-290
Carmarthen Royal Field (Reserve) Artillery *formerly* Carmarthen Royal Rifles Militia	WO 68/3-22
Cavan Militia *became* 4th Bn Royal Irish Fusiliers	WO 68/402-405
Cheshire Regiment, 4th Bn *formerly* Cheshire 2nd Royal Militia	WO 68/214
Clare Royal Field (Reserve) Artillery *formerly* Clare Militia	WO 68/23

Connaught Rangers, 3rd Bn *formerly* North and South Mayo Militia *and* Galway Militia	WO 68/319-328 WO 79/1
Connaught Rangers, 5th Bn *formerly* Roscommon Militia	WO 68/475 WO 79/41, 44-45
Cork City Artillery Militia	WO 68/368
Cork City Infantry Militia *became* Royal Munster Fusiliers	WO 68/409
Cork, North, Infantry Militia *became* 9th Bn King's Royal Rifle Corps	WO 68/306-312
Cornwall and Devon Miners Royal Field (Reserve) Artillery *formerly* Cornwall and Devon Miners Artillery Militia	WO 68/24-25
Cumberland Militia, Royal *became* 3rd Bn Border Regiment	WO 68/376
Devon Royal Field (Reserve) Artillery *formerly* Devon Artillery Militia	WO 68/26-27
Devon, Cornwall and Miners Royal Field (Reserve) Artillery *formerly* Devon, Cornwall and Miners Artillery Militia	WO 68/24-25
Devon 2nd or South Militia *became* Devonshire Regiment, 3rd Bn	WO 68/139, 306-312
Donegal Royal Field (Reserve) Artillery *formerly* Donegal Artillery Militia	WO 68/28-30
Donegal Militia *became* 5th Bn Royal Inniskilling Fusiliers	WO 68/221-230
Dublin City Royal Field (Reserve) Artillery *formerly* Dublin City Artillery Militia	WO 68/31-32
Dublin Fusiliers, 4th Bn *formerly* Dublin City Militia	WO 68/491

Dumfries Militia *became* 3rd Bn King's Own Scottish Borderers	WO 68/508
Durham Royal Field (Reserve) Artillery *formerly* Durham Artillery Militia	WO 68/33-34
Edinburgh County Militia *became* 3rd Bn Royal Scots (Lothian) Regiment	WO 68/551-561
Edinburgh Royal Field (Reserve) Artillery *formerly* Edinburgh Artillery Militia	WO 68/35-40
Essex Regiment, 4th Bn *formerly* Essex West Militia	WO 68/257-277, 359-360
Fermanagh Militia *became* 3rd Bn Royal Inniskilling Fusiliers	WO 68/382
Fife Royal Field (Reserve) Artillery *formerly* Fife Militia	WO 68/41
Forfar and Kincardine Royal Field (Reserve) Artillery *formerly* Forfar and Kincardine Militia	WO 68/42-43
Galway Militia *became* 3rd Bn Connaught Rangers	WO 68/328 WO 79/1
Glamorgan Royal (Reserve) Artillery *formerly* Glamorgan Artillery Militia	WO 68/44 WO 69/612
Gloucester Regiment, 4th Bn *formerly* Gloucester Royal North Militia	WO 68/231-241 WO 76/266
Gordon Highlanders, 3rd Bn *formerly* Royal Aberdeenshire Militia	WO 76/451-452
Haddington Artillery Militia *became part of* South East of Scotland Royal Field (Reserve) Artillery	WO 68/78-85
Hampshire Regiment, 3rd Bn *formerly* Hampshire Militia	WO 68/379-381 WO 76/518

Hampshire and Isle of Wight Royal Field (Reserve) Artillery *formerly* Hampshire and Isle of Wight Artillery Militia	WO 68/45-53
Hereford Militia *became* 4th Bn Shropshire Light Infantry	WO 68/278-295
Hertfordshire Militia *became* 4th Bn Bedfordshire Regiment	WO 68/375
Highland Light Infantry, Inverness and, Militia *became* 3rd Bn Cameron Highlanders	WO 68/378
Highland Light Infantry, 3rd Bn *formerly* 1st Royal Lanark Regiment	WO 68/503-506, 522
Highland Light Infantry, 4th Bn	WO 68/489-490
Inniskilling Fusiliers, Royal, 3rd Bn *formerly* Fermanagh Militia	WO 68/382
Inniskilling Fusiliers, Royal, 4th Bn *formerly* Royal Tyrone Infantry Militia	WO 68/71,382
Inniskilling Fusiliers, Royal, 5th Bn *formerly* Donegal Militia	WO 68/221-230
Inniskilling Fusiliers, Royal, 6th Bn *not identified*	WO 68/382
Inverness and Highland Light Infantry Militia *became* 3rd Bn Cameron Highlanders	WO 68/378
Irish Fusiliers, Royal, 3rd Bn *formerly* Armagh Militia	WO 68/383-401
Irish Fusiliers, Royal, 4th Bn *formerly* Cavan Militia	WO 68/402-405
Irish Fusiliers, Royal, 5th Bn *formerly* Monaghan Militia	WO 68/316-318
Irish Regiment, Royal, 3rd Bn *formerly* Wexford Militia	WO 68/173-174

Irish Rifles, Royal, 6th Bn *formerly* Louth Militia	WO 68/313-315
Kent Royal Field (Reserve) Artillery *formerly* Kent Artillery Militia	WO 68/337-340
Kent, Royal West Regiment, 3rd Bn *formerly* Kent West Light Infantry Militia	WO 68/406
Kerry Militia *became* 4th Bn Royal Munster Fusiliers	WO 68/410-412
Kilkenny Militia	WO 68/456-457
Kincardine, Forfar and Royal Field (Reserve) Artillery *formerly* Kincardine and Forfar Artillery Militia	WO 68/42-43
King's County Militia *became* 3rd Bn Leinster Regiment	WO 68/408
King's Own Light Infantry Militia *became* 3rd Bn King's Own Infantry Brigade	WO 68/407, 416-438
King's Own Yorkshire Light Infantry, 3rd Bn *formerly* 1st West Yorkshire Militia	WO 68/448, 474, 499(1)
King's (Liverpool) Regiment, 3rd and 4th Bn *formerly* 2nd Lancashire Regiment	WO 68/488
King's Royal Rifle Corps, 8th Bn *formerly* Carlow Militia	WO 68/296-305 WO 79/289-290
King's Royal Rifle Corps, 9th Bn *formerly* North Cork Infantry Militia	WO 68/306-312
Lanark, 1st Royal Regiment *became* 3rd Bn Highland Light Infantry	WO 68/503-506, 522
Lancashire, 1st, 2nd and 3rd Batteries, Royal Field (Reserve) Artillery *formerly* Lancashire Royal Field Artillery Militia	WO 68/54-58 WO 76/160-162

Lancashire, 2nd Regiment *became* 3rd or 4th Bn King's (Liverpool) Regiment	WO 68/488
Lancashire Fusiliers, 3rd Bn *formerly* 7th Lancashire Rifles	WO 68/500
Lancashire Militia, Amounderness Bn	WO 79/2
Lancaster Regiment, 1st Royal	WO 68/479
Leinster Regiment, 3rd Bn *formerly* King's County Militia	WO 68/408
Limerick Royal Field (Reserve) Artillery *formerly* Limerick City Militia	WO 68/59-63
Lincoln Militia, Royal South *became* 4th Bn Lincolnshire Regiment	WO 68/131-138
Lincoln Militia, Royal North *became* 3rd Bn Lincolnshire Regiment	WO 68/458-462
Linlithgow Artillery Militia *became* part of South East of Scotland Royal Field (Reserve) Artillery	WO 68/78-85
Liverpool Regiment *see* King's (Liverpool) Regiment	
Londonderry Royal Field (Reserve) Artillery *formerly* Londonderry Artillery Militia *formerly* Londonderry Light Infantry Militia	WO 68/64-67
Longford and Westmeath Militia, Royal *became on amalgamation* 6th Bn Rifle Brigade, *prior to amalgamation were respectively* 9th and 6th Bn Rifle Brigade	WO 68/329-336, 439 WO 76/286, 292
Louth Militia *became* 6th Bn Royal Irish Rifles	WO 68/313-315
Mayo North Militia and Mayo South Militia *amalgamated and became* 3rd Bn Connaught Rangers	WO 68/319-328
Medway Division, Royal Engineers	WO 68/369

Merioneth Militia, Royal Caernarvon and, *became* 4th Bn Royal Welch Fusiliers   WO 68/215-217

Mid-Ulster Royal Field (Reserve) Artillery *formerly* Tyrone Artillery Militia   WO 68/68-72

Monaghan Militia *became* 5th Bn Royal Irish Fusiliers   WO 68/316-318

Monmouthshire Bn   WO 68/507

Monmouth Militia, Royal   WO 25/3920

Montgomery Militia, Royal *became* 4th Bn South Wales Borderers   WO 68/218-220, 450-455

Munster Fusiliers, Royal *formerly* Cork City Infantry Militia (not identified)   WO 68/409

Munster Fusiliers, Royal, 4th Bn *formerly* Kerry Militia   WO 68/410-412

Norfolk Royal Field (Reserve) Artillery *formerly* Norfolk Artillery Militia   WO 68/341-345

Norfolk Regiment, 4th Bn *formerly* 2nd or East Norfolk Militia   WO 68/123-130, 498

Norfolk Militia, West   WO 68/467-469

Northumberland Royal Field (Reserve) Artillery *formerly* Northumberland Artillery Militia   WO 68/73,121

Oxford Militia *became* 4th Bn Oxfordshire Light Infantry   WO 68/413-414

Oxfordshire Light Infantry, 3rd Bn *formerly* Royal Buckinghamshire Militia   WO 68/242-256

Peeblesshire Artillery Militia *became* part of South East of Scotland Royal Field (Reserve) Artillery   WO 68/78-85

Pembroke Royal Field (Reserve) Artillery *formerly* Pembroke Artillery Militia	WO 68/74-75
Plymouth Division, Royal Engineers	WO 68/370
Portsmouth Division, Royal Engineers	WO 68/371
Queen's Own Light Infantry Militia *became* 5th Bn Rifle Brigade	WO 68/415
Renfrew Militia, Royal *became* 4th Bn Argyll and Sutherland Highlanders	WO 68/372-374
Rifle Brigade, 5th Bn *formerly* Queen's Own Royal Tower Hamlets Militia	WO 68/415
Rifle Brigade, 6th Bn *formerly* Royal Longford and Westmeath Militia	WO 68/329-336
Rifle Brigade, 7th Bn *formerly* King's Own Royal Tower Hamlets Militia	WO 68/407, 416-438
Rifle Brigade, 9th Bn *formerly* Royal Westmeath Militia *became* part of 6th Bn	WO 68/439
Rifle Corps, King's Royal, 8th Bn *formerly* Carlow Militia	WO 68/296-305
Rifle Corps, King's Royal, 9th Bn *formerly* North Cork Infantry Militia	WO 68/306-312
Roscommon Militia *became* 5th Bn Connaught Rangers	WO 68/475
Royal Tyrone Infantry Militia *became* 4th Bn Royal Inniskilling Fusiliers	WO 68/71,382
Scotland, South East of, Royal Field (Reserve) Artillery *formerly* Berwick, Haddington, Linlithgow and Peeblesshire Artillery Militia	WO 68/78-85
Scotland, West of, Royal Field (Reserve) Artillery *formerly* Argyll and Bute Artillery Militia	WO 68/98-117

Scots (Lothian) Regiment, Royal, 3rd Bn *formerly* Edinburgh County Militia	WO 68/551-561
Scottish Borderers, 3rd Bn King's Own *formerly* Dumfries Militia	WO 68/508
Shropshire Light Infantry, 4th Bn *formerly* Hereford Militia	WO 68/278-295
Shropshire Militia (King's) *became* 3rd Bn Shropshire Light Infantry	WO 68/440
Sligo Royal Field (Reserve) Artillery *formerly* Sligo Artillery Militia	WO 68/76-77
Somerset Light Infantry, 3rd and 4th Bn *formerly* 1st and 2nd Somerset Militia	WO 68/441-444
Somerset Light Infantry, 4th Bn only *formerly* 2nd Somerset Militia	WO 68/158-172
Somerset, 1st and 2nd Militia *became* 3rd and 4th Bn Somerset Light Infantry	(see previous 2 references)
South Wales Borderers, 4th Bn *formerly* Royal Montgomery Militia	WO 68/218-220, 450-455
Staffordshire Regiment, South, 3rd and 4th Bn *formerly* Stafford Militia, 1st King's Own	WO 68/523-534
Staffordshire Regiment, North, 3rd and 4th Bn *formerly* Stafford Militia, 2nd and 3rd King's Own	WO 68/470-471
Suffolk Royal Field (Reserve) Artillery *formerly* Suffolk Artillery Militia *formerly* East Suffolk Light Infantry Militia	WO 68/348-358
Suffolk Regiment, 2nd Bn	WO 68/480-482
Suffolk Regiment, 3rd Bn *formerly* Suffolk Militia, West	WO 68/463-466, 492-494, 509-514, 516-521, 549

Suffolk Regiment, 4th Bn *formerly* Cambridge Militia	WO 68/140-157
Surrey Regiment, East, 3rd and 4th Bn *formerly* 1st and 3rd Royal Surrey Militia	WO 68/445 WO 76/64,65,68
Surrey Regiment, West, 3rd Bn *formerly* 2nd Royal Surrey Militia	WO 68/477-478
Sussex Royal Field (Reserve) Artillery *formerly* Royal Sussex Artillery Militia	WO 68/86-87
Tipperary Royal Field (Reserve) Artillery *formerly* 1st or South Artillery Militia	WO 68/88-95
Tower Hamlets, 1st or King's Own Royal Militia *became* 7th Bn Rifle Brigade	WO 68/407, 416-438
Tower Hamlets, 2nd or Queen's Own Royal Militia *became* 5th Bn Rifle Brigade	WO 68/415 WO 76/285
Tyrone Artillery Militia *became* Mid-Ulster Royal Field (Reserve) Artillery	WO 68/68-72
Ulster, Mid-, Royal Field (Reserve) Artillery *formerly* Tyrone Artillery Militia	WO 68/68-72
Wales Borderers, South, 4th Bn *formerly* Royal Montgomery Militia	WO 68/218-220, 450-455
Warwick Regiment, 4th Bn *formerly* 2nd Warwick Militia	WO 68/361-367
Waterford Royal Field (Reserve) Artillery *formerly* Waterford Artillery Militia	WO 68/96-97
Welch Fusiliers, Royal, 4th Bn *formerly* Royal Caernarvon and Merioneth Militia	WO 68/215-217
West Riding Regiment, 3rd Bn *formerly* 6th West Yorkshire Militia	WO 68/215-217

West of Scotland Royal Field (Reserve) Artillery *formerly* Argyll and Bute Artillery Militia — WO 68/98-117

Westmeath Militia, Royal *amalgamated* Westmeath and Royal Longford Militia *became* 9th Bn Rifle Brigade *later became part of* 6th Bn Rifle Brigade — WO 68/329-336, 439 / WO 76/286,292

Westmorland Militia, Royal *became* 4th Bn Border Regiment — WO 68/377

Wexford Militia *became* 3rd Bn Royal Irish Regiment — WO 68/173-174

Wicklow Royal Field (Reserve) Artillery *formerly* Wicklow Artillery Militia *formerly* Wicklow Rifle Militia — WO 68/118-120

Wight, Isle of, and Hampshire Royal Field (Reserve) Artillery *formerly* Wight, Isle of, and Hampshire Artillery Militia — WO 68/34-53

Wiltshire Militia, 5th Bn — WO 79/24 / WO 76/530

Worcestershire Militia *became* 3rd Bn Worcestershire Regiment — WO 76/493

York, East and North, Artillery Militia *became* Yorkshire Royal Field (Reserve) Artillery — WO 68/121-122

York and Lancaster Regiment, 3rd Bn *formerly* 3rd West Yorkshire Militia — WO 68/447,473, 499

Yorkshire, North, Militia *became* 4th Bn Yorkshire Regiment — WO 68/175-213

Yorkshire, 1st West, Militia *became* 3rd Bn King's Own Yorkshire Light Infantry — WO 68/448, 474, 499(1)

Yorkshire, 2nd West, Militia *became* 3rd Bn West Yorkshire Regiment — WO 68/449 / WO 76/316

Yorkshire, 3rd West, Militia *became* 3rd Bn York and Lancaster Regiment	WO 68/447,473, 499
Yorkshire, 4th West, Militia *became* 4th Bn West Yorkshire Regiment	WO 76/316
Yorkshire, 5th West, Militia *became* 3rd Bn Yorkshire Regiment	WO 68/535-546
Yorkshire, 6th West, Militia *became* 3rd Bn West Riding Regiment	WO 68/446
Yorkshire Regiment, 3rd Bn *formerly* 5th West York Militia	WO 68/535-546
Yorkshire Light Infantry, King's Own 3rd Bn *formerly* 1st West Yorkshire Militia	WO 68/448,474, 499(1)
Yorkshire Regiment, 4th Bn *formerly* North Yorkshire Militia	WO 68/175-213
Yorkshire, West, Regiment, 3rd Bn *formerly* 2nd West Yorkshire Militia	WO 68/449
Yorkshire Royal Field (Reserve) Artillery *formerly* East and North York Artillery Militia	WO 68/121-122
Yorkshire, South, Regiment *became* King's Own Yorkshire Light Infantry	WO 68/448

APPENDIX 4

IMPERIAL YEOMANRY COMPANIES AND BATTALIONS

Each company of the Imperial Yeomanry was given a name, usually the county from where the men enlisted but in some cases more flamboyant names. The names, where known, are listed below. Each company of the Imperial Yeomanry was placed into a battalion. In most cases a company stayed in the same battalion for the duration of its service in South Africa. Unless otherwise stated the first or only battalion number was the battalion in which the company served in both 1900 and 1901. If a company changed battalions, the first number is for 1900, the second for 1901.

Company	Name or Title	Battalion
1	Wiltshire	1
2	Wiltshire	1
3	Gloucestershire	1
4	Glamorganshire	1
5	Warwickshire	2
6	Staffordshire	4
7	Leicestershire	4
8	Derbyshire	4
9	Yorkshire	3
10	Sherwood Rangers	3
11	Yorkshire	3
12	South Notts	3
13	Shropshire	5
14	Northumberland	5
15	Northumberland	5
16	Worcestershire	5
17	Ayrshire	6
18	Queen's Own Royal Glasgow	6
19	Lothian	6
20	Fife and Forfar Light Horse	6
21	Cheshire	2
22	Cheshire	2
23	Lancashire	8
24	Westmorland and Cumberland	8
25	West Somerset	7
26	Dorsetshire	7
27	Devonshire	7
28	Bedfordshire	4
29	Denbighshire	9
30	Pembrokeshire	9
31	Montgomeryshire	9
32	Lancashire	2

Company	Name or Title	Battalion
33	Royal East Kent	11
34	Middlesex	11
35	Middlesex	11
36	West Kent	9
37	Buckinghamshire	10
38	Buckinghamshire	10
39	Berkshire	10
40	Oxfordshire	10
41	Hampshire	12 & 4
42	Hertfordshire	12
43	Suffolk	12
44	Suffolk	12
45	Dublin	13 (1900 service only)
46	Belfast	13
47	Duke of Cambridge's Own	13 (1900 service only)
48	North Somerset	7
49	Montgomeryshire	9
51	Paget's Horse	8
52	Paget's Horse	19 (1900 service only)
53	Royal East Kent	14 & 11
55	Northumberland	14 & 5
56	Buckinghamshire	15
57	Buckinghamshire	15
58	Berkshire	15
59	Oxfordshire	15
60	North Irish Horse	17
61	South Irish Horse	17
62	Middlesex	14 & 11
63	Wiltshire	16 & 1
65	Leicestershire	17
66	Yorkshire	16 & 3
67	Sharpshooters	18
68	Paget's Horse	19 (1900 service only)
69	Sussex	14 & 7
70	Sharpshooters	18
71	Sharpshooters	18
72	Rough Riders	20 (1900 service only)
73	Paget's Horse	19 & 12
74	Dublin	16 & 8
75	Sharpshooters	18
76	Rough Riders	20 & 22
77	Manchester	8
78	Rough Riders	20 & 22
79	Rough Riders	20 (1900 service only)

Company	Name or Title	Battalion
	The following companies only served in 1901	
80	Sharpshooters	21
81	Sharpshooters	21
82	Sharpshooters	21
83	Sharpshooters	21
84	Rough Riders	22
85	Rough Riders	22
86	Rough Riders	24
87	Rough Riders	24
88	Welsh Yeomanry	9
89	Montgomeryshire	9
90	Sharpshooters	23
93	Sharpshooters	23
94	Metropolitan Mounted Rifles	24
95	Metropolitan Mounted Rifles	24
96	Metropolitan Mounted Rifles	24
97	Metropolitan Mounted Rifles	24
100	Northumberland	5
101	Northumberland	5
102	Worcestershire	5
103	Warwickshire	2
104	Derbyshire	4
105	Manchester	8
106	Staffordshire	4
107	Lanarkshire	6
108	Royal Glasgow	6
109	Yorkshire Hussars	3
110	Northumberland	2
111	Yorkshire Dragoons	3
112	Middlesex	11
113	Served with Lovats Scouts	
114	Served with Lovats Scouts	
115	Sharpshooters	25
116		25
117	Sharpshooters	25
118	Sharpshooters	25
119		26
120	Younghusband's Horse	26
121		26
122		26
123		27
124		27
125		27
126		27

Company	Name or Title	Battalion
127	Westminster Dragoons	28
128	Westminster Dragoons	28
129	Westminster Dragoons	28
130	Westminster Dragoons	28
131	Irish Horse	29
132	Irish Horse	29
133	Irish Horse	29
134	Irish Horse	29
135		30
136		30
137		30
138		30
139	Fincastle's Horse	31
140	Fincastle's Horse	31
141	Fincastle's Horse	31
142	Fincastle's Horse	31
143		32
144		32
145		32
146		32
147		33
148		33
149		33
150		33
151		34
152		34
153		34
154		34
155		35
156		35
157		35
158		35
159		36
160		36
161		36
162		36
163		37
164		37
165		37
166		37
167		38
168		38
169		38
170		38
171		39

Company	Name or Title	Battalion
172		39
173		39
174		39
175	Irish Horse	29
176	Irish Horse	29
177		31

Source WO 100/120 f 2 and April 1902 *Army List.*

APPENDIX 5

HOME GUARD UNIT HISTORIES

2 Battalion Anglesey Home Guard, 1940-1945	WO 199/3311
Ayrshire Home Guard, 1940-1945	WO 199/3312
2 Battalion Bedfordshire Home Guard, 1940-1945	WO 199/3313
6 (Bracknell) Battalion Berkshire Home Guard, 1940-1945	WO 199/3314
B (Sandhurst) Coy 11 Battalion Berkshire Home Guard, 1940-1945	WO 199/3315
35 Battalion Cheshire Home Guard, 1940-1945	WO 199/3316
3 Battalion Derbyshire Home Guard, 1940-1945	WO 199/3309
9 Derby/Notts Anti-Aircraft Regiment, 1942-1945	WO 199/3310
7 Battalion Denbigh and Flint Home Guard, 1940-1945	WO 199/3317
6 Battalion Devonshire Home Guard, 1940-1945	WO 199/3318
10 (Torbay) Battalion Devonshire Home Guard, 1940-1945	WO 199/3319
2 Battalion Dumbarton Home Guard, 1940-1945	WO 199/3320
101 (Dumbarton) Anti-Aircraft Rocket Battery, 1940-1945	WO 199/3321
1 Battalion Dumfries-shire Home Guard, 1940-1945	WO 199/3322
3 (13 GPO) City of Dundee Home Guard, 1940-1945	WO 199/3323
2 Battalion Durham Home Guard, 1940-1945	WO 199/3324
9 Battalion City of Edinburgh Home Guard, 1940-1945	WO 199/3325
102 (City of Edinburgh) Anti-Aircraft Rocket Battery, 1940-1945	WO 199/3326
3 Battalion Essex Home Guard, 1940-1945	WO 199/3327
19 Battalion Essex Home Guard, 1940-1945	WO 199/3328
196 (102 Essex HG) Anti-Aircraft Rocket Battery, 1940-1945	WO 199/3329
1, 6,7,9,10, 12 & 13 Battalions City of Glasgow Home Guard, 1940-1945	WO 199/3330
2 Battalion City of Glasgow Home Guard, 1940-1945	WO 199/3331
3 Battalion City of Glasgow Home Guard, 1940-1945	WO 199/3332
14 (City of Bristol) Gloucestershire Home Guard, 1940-1945	WO 199/3333
3 (Basingstoke) Hampshire Home Guard, 1940-1945	WO 199/3334
A (Winchester City) Coy, 5 Battalion Hampshire Home Guard, 1940-1945	WO 199/3335
Electricity Coy, 17 (Portsmouth) Battalion Hampshire Home Guard, 1940-1945	WO 199/3336
18 (Dockyard Portsmouth) Battalion Hampshire Home Guard, 1940-1945	WO 199/3337
23 Battalion Hampshire Home Guard, 1940-1945	WO 199/3338
29 (Gosport) Battalion Hampshire Home Guard, 1940-1945	WO 199/3339
32 (Connaught) Battalion Hampshire Home Guard, 1940-1945	WO 199/3340

71 (Hants and Isle of Wight) HAA Bty, 1940-1945	WO 199/3341
3 Battalion Huntingdonshire Home Guard, 1940-1945	WO 199/3342
5 (Wingham) Battalion Kent Home Guard, 1940-1945	WO 199/3343
16 (Kent) Anti-Aircraft Regt, 1940-1945	WO 199/3344
19 (Farningham) Battalion Kent Home Guard, 1940-1945	WO 199/3202, 3345
20 (Sevenoaks) Battalion Kent Home Guard, 1940-1945	WO 199/3346
22 (Tunbridge Wells) Battalion Kent Home Guard, 1940-1945	WO 199/3201
42 Battalion County of Lancaster Home Guard, 1940-1945	WO 199/3347
101 (Leicestershire) Anti-Aircraft Rocket Bty, 1940-1945	WO 199/3348
6 (Silvertown) Battalion City/County of London Home Guard, 1940-1945	WO 199/3349
19 (South Suburban Gas Co) Battalion City/County of London Home Guard, 1940-1945	WO199/3350
40 (GLCC) Battalion City/County of London Home Guard, 1940-1945	WO 199/3352
44 (London Transport) Battalion City/County of London Home Guard, 1940-1945	WO 199/3353
48 (LCC) Battalion City/County of London Home Guard, 1940-1945	WO 199/3354
59 (Taxi) Battalion City/County of London Home Guard, 1940-1945	WO 199/3355
2 (Newport) Battalion Monmouthshire Home Guard, 1940-1945	WO 199/3356
10 Battalion Monmouthshire Home Guard, 1940-1945	WO 199/3357
101 (Monmouthshire) Anti-Aircraft Rocket Bty, 1940-1945	WO 199/3358
101 (Northamptonshire) Anti-Aircraft Rocket Bty, 1940-1945	WO 199/3359
2 (Bicester) Battalion Oxfordshire Home Guard, 1940-1945	WO 199/3360
4 (Bullingdon) Battalion Oxfordshire Home Guard, 1940-1945	WO 199/3361
102 (Renfrewshire) Anti-Aircraft Rocket Bty, 1940-1945	WO 199/3362
1 Scottish Border Battalion Home Guard, March 1944	WO 199/3207
2 Scottish Border Battalion Home Guard, December 1942	WO 199/3208
7 Battalion Somerset Home Guard, 1940-1945	WO 199/3363
2 Coy, 7 Battalion Somerset Home Guard, 1940-1945	WO 199/3364
8 (Burton) Battalion Staffordshire Home Guard, 1945	WO 199/3206
13 Battalion North Staffordshire Home Guard, 1940-1945	WO 199/3365
11 Battalion Suffolk Home Guard, 1940-1945	WO 199/3366
4 (Guildford) Battalion Surrey Home Guard, 1940-1945	WO 199/3367
8 (Reigate) Battalion Surrey Home Guard, 1940-1945	WO 199/3368
53 Battalion Surrey Home Guard, 1940-1945	WO 199/3369
58 Battalion Surrey Home Guard, 1940-1945	WO 199/3370
63 (Richmond) Battalion Surrey Home Guard, 1940-1945	WO 199/3371
West Sussex Group, August 1945	WO 199/3203

Sussex Recovery Coy, 1940-1945	WO 199/3373
1 (Chichester) Battalion Sussex Home Guard, June 1945	WO 199/3204
11 (GPO) Battalion Sussex Home Guard, 1940-1945	WO 199/3372
26 (Worth Forest) Battalion Sussex Home Guard, 1940-1945	WO 199/3205
A Sector 2 & 7 Battalions Warwickshire Home Guard, 1940-1945	WO 199/3374
31 & 32 (Birmingham City Transport) Battalions Warwickshire HG, 1940-1945	WO 199/3375
45 (Birmingham) Battalion Warwickshire Home Guard, 1940-1945	WO 199/3376
1 (Bradford) Battalion West Riding Home Guard, 1940-1945	WO 199/3377
16 (GPO) Battalion West Riding Home Guard, 1940-1945	WO 199/3378
A Coy, 4 Battalion Wiltshire Home Guard, 1940-1945	WO 199/3379
9 Battalion Wiltshire Home Guard, 1940-1945	WO 199/3380
4 (Evesham) Battalion Worcestershire Home Guard, 1940-1945	WO 199/ 3381, 3382
12 (Warley) Battalion Worcestershire Home Guard, 1940-1945	WO 199/3383
1 Zetland Battalion Home Guard, January-March 1942	WO 199/3209

APPENDIX 6

SOME ADDRESSES OF RECORD REPOSITORIES OUTSIDE THE PUBLIC RECORD OFFICE

A. Local Authority Record Offices

Reference has been made in this guide to the fact or possibility that certain records have or may have been placed in county or other local authority record offices. Details of the holdings of each, and information about opening times and addresses, can be found in J Foster and J Sheppard, *British Archives: A Guide to Archive Resources in the United Kingdom,* 2nd edn, London, 1995. In briefer form, similar information is found in *Record Repositories in Great Britain,* (1997 edition forthcoming, PRO Publications).

B. Military Museums

B.1 Imperial War Museum

With particular responsibility for material records, written records of a non-official type (private papers, letters, diaries) and captured enemy records, left by the wars of this century, together with a substantial library of printed works, is the

> Imperial War Museum
> Lambeth Road
> London
> SE1 6HZ

where researchers are welcome following preliminary enquiry (0171-416-5000).

B.2 National Army Museum

Having wider responsibility and holdings is the

> National Army Museum
> Royal Hospital Road
> London
> SW3 4HT.

The museum mounts displays of material documents left by military engagements that have involved Great Britain. It possesses an important library of printed works together with some copies of public records. It is accessible to researchers following preliminary enquiry (0171-730-0717).

B.3 Regimental Museums

Most regiments have established a museum, holding material records and non-public records and in some cases public records. Their addresses are listed in T Wise, *A Guide to Military Museums,* Terence Wise, 1994.

C. Office of Population Censuses and Surveys

C.1 England and Wales

Records of the civil registration of births, marriages and deaths that have occurred in England and Wales since 1 July 1837, are in the custody of the

> Office for National Statistics
> Family Records Centre
> 1 Myddelton Street
> London
> EC1R 1UW

where researchers in person have access to the lists and order copies of certificates.

Written applications, on the other hand, should be addressed to the

> Office for National Statistics
>   (General Register Office)
> Postal Application Section
> Smedley Hydro
> Trafalgar Road
> Birkdale
> Southport
> Merseyside
> PR8 2HH.

C.2 Scotland

Similar records pertaining particularly to Scotland and Scottish military personnel are held at the

> General Register Office for Scotland
> New Register House
> Edinburgh
> EH1 3YT.

C.3 Republic of Ireland

Similar records pertaining to Ireland and, since 1920, to the Republic of Ireland (Eire), are held at the

> General Register Office
> Joyce House
> 8-11 Lombard Street
> Dublin 2
> Republic of Ireland.

D. Scottish Record Office

Documents described in the text as preserved in the SRO are held at

> Scottish Record Office
> HM General Register House
> Edinburgh
> EH1 3YY.

E. Society of Genealogists

Help in tracing surviving records of militia ancestors may also be obtained from the

> Society of Genealogists
> 14 Charterhouse Buildings
> Goswell Road
> London
> EC1M 7BA
> (0171-251-8799).

F. Ministry of Defence Departments

For post 1920 records of service

F.1   Ministry of Defence
                           CS (R) 2b
                           Bourne Avenue
                           Hayes
                           Middlesex
                           UB3 1RF

For post 1920 campaign medals and Home Guard records of service

F.2   Army Medal Office
                           Goverment Office Buildings
                           Worcester Road
                           Droitwich
                           Worcestershire
                           WR9 8AU

G. Commonwealth War Graves Commission

                           2 Marlow Road
                           Maidenhead
                           Berkshire
                           SL6 7DX

INDEX

V

W

Y